# Hawai'i

# A Photographer's Guide to the Big Island

## Being in the Right Place, at the Right Time, for the Best Image!

Robert Frutos

One of Hawai'i's best known
Nature Photographers & Camera Artist's

Text by Robert Frutos



ISBN-13: 978-1499675290 ePub ISBN-10: 1499675291

**Also by Robert Frutos;**

A Photographer's Guide to Hawai'i Volcanoes National Park: Being in the Right Place, at the Right time, for the Best Image!

Day Hikes in Hawai'i Volcanoes National Park: The Best Places to See the Unusual, Find the Unexpected, and Experience the Magnificent!

Hawai'i the Most Beautiful Places to Visit on the Big Island!

Hawai'i Sacred Sites of the Big Island Places of Presence, Healing & Wisdom

*See full list of titles by Robert Frutos on Page 101*

**www.hawaiiphototours.org**

**www.hawaiisacredsitestours.com**

**www.robertfrutos.com**

**email: rfphoto3@gmail.com Phone: 808 345 – 7179**

# Dedication

To those who have come to experience and capture the magnificent beauty and wonder of the Big Island, yet find themselves with little time to visit…

and for those of you who have the luxury of a longer stay…

this guidebook shares the most beautiful places to capture images on the Big Island, and how to easily access them.

**This book is for you!**

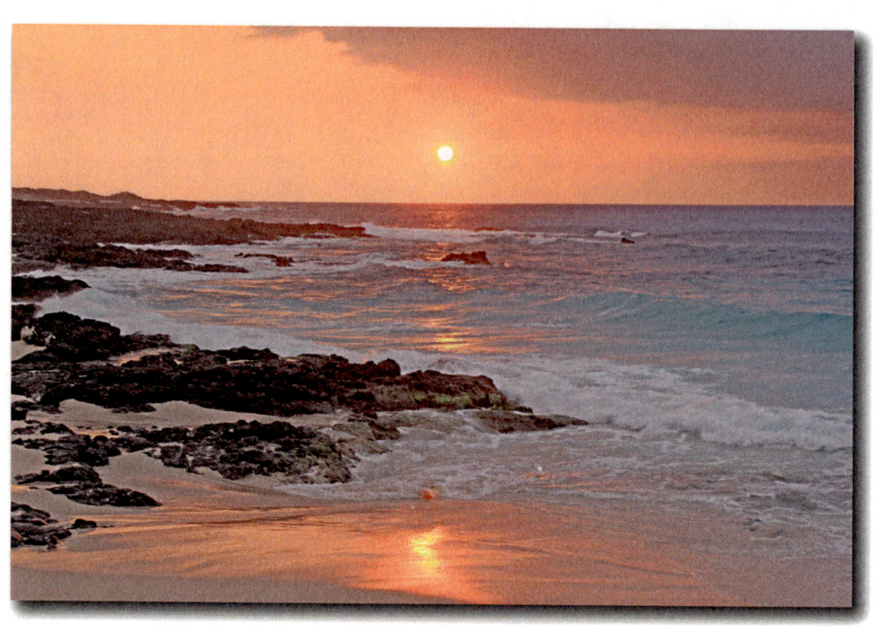

**Kua Bay, Sunset**

All Images by Robert Frutos

# Table of Context

# Preface

**Hawai'i is truly one of the planet's most fascinating natural wonders -** with pristine beaches, warm tropical breezes, turquoise waters, gently swaying palms, magnificent waterfalls, endless rainbows and an active volcano. Hawai'i offers a unique and unforgettable photographic experience.

While all the Hawaiian Islands have their own unique beauty and stunning vistas, with cultural hues and flavors, the Big Island of Hawai'i retains its own remarkable wealth of unique, unexpected, and magnificent features.

Through time, the Big Island has developed its own multi-colored flora and fauna. Its own distinctive and unusual evolution of life… with unceasing lava flows, vast bio-diverse forests, and a nearly 14,000 ft. high mountain. It also has it own endemic species of birds, insects, and sea life.

The Big Island of Hawai'i contains one the worlds greatest concentrations of climate types. From dry, coastal, desert strand to some of the wettest spots on earth, from warm humid tropical lushness to stark, barren, snow - capped mountains, the Big Island offers an astonishing array of photographic opportunities.

Perhaps, because it is the biggest island that vast tracts of open land remain virtually untouched and accessible (all the other islands put together fit into its footprint.)

It is for these reasons that I choose to make the Big Island my home. And because I am foremost a camera artist/nature photographer, I have spent untold hours, days, months and years - exploring and discovering the many unique features and diverse areas of the Big Island, including the little-known, rarely visited, remote locations, as well as the more easily accessible.

And, of course, on any photo adventure on the Big Island - one *must* include the magnificent **Hawai'i Volcanoes National Park.** Here you will find surreal lavascapes, the spectacular pluming Halema'uma'u Crater, spewing steam vents, the wild Puna Coast, over 150 miles of hiking trails, and a lit lava tube with easy access.

Whether the crater is pluming, and the lava is flowing, or not, **Hawai'i Volcanoes National Park will be one of the most captivating places you will ever visit.**

For specific photo information regarding the park, I have another book available entitled **A Photographer's Guide to Hawai'i Volcanoes National Park: Being in the Right Place, at the Right Time, for the Best Image!**

**The Big Island of Hawai'i is such a Fabulous Place...** not only for the extraordinary beauty and magnificence of the sweeping views and tropical panoramas, but for the phenomenal spirit that pervades the native culture, and the traditions that keep them thriving.

A spirit (known as the Aloha Spirit) is felt, both in the love and liveliness of its people, AND as a *living breathing vitality* that permeates the landscape.

**And it's all here just waiting for you – All you have to do to capture that potential once in a lifetime image -** ***is allow the great wonder and beauty to inspire you, set your camera options (see "A Word About the Camera") -and let your creativity and imagination flow.***

# A Note About the Creation of this Book...

This book was created by request.
A number of individuals and photographers approached me after reading: **A Photographer's Guide to Hawai'i Volcanoes National Park: Being in the Right Place, at the Right Time, for the Best Image!**

They asked me to write a book specifically oriented to capturing images of the most beautiful places on the Big Island, after finding the first book so valuable and easy to use.

**Hawai'i A Photographer's Guide to the Big Island** is the result. It contains information towards capturing potential once-in-a-lifetime images on the Big Island, inspiring images to share what is possible, and easily accessible locations with directions.

Moreover, if your passion is creating successful and dynamic images while visiting the Big Island – I highly recommend my other book - **Hawaii How to Capture the Dynamic Islandscape: A Photographers Approach**.

It shares in-depth information both about the camera itself (how to make adjustments for optimizing the camera for your specific use) and valuable insights, about the process and steps I use to capture my own extraordinary images.

Lastly, I have one more photography book available, an inspiring coffee table book entitled: **Hawaii Inspiration Aflame: A Passion for the Magnificence**, for those who would like to see more extraordinary Hawai'i images, it includes images from some of the other Hawai'i islands as well. This book is available directly from the author and the cost is $65.00, plus shipping. Email me at rfphoto3@gmail.com for more info. or to obtain a copy.

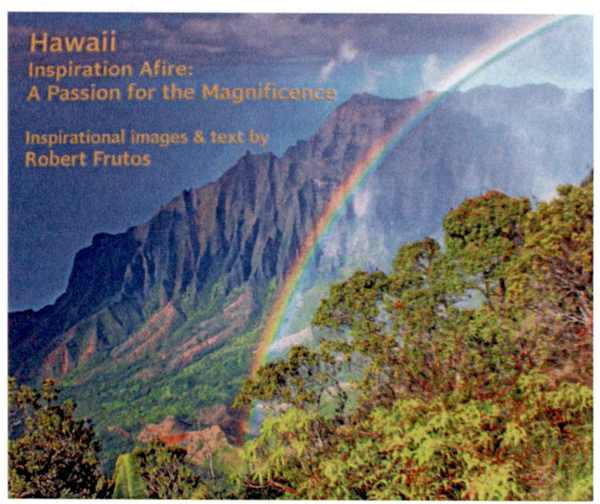


**If you are here, for one or many fun-filled photo adventures, full of the wondrous, the beautiful and the magnificent, then Hawai'i A Photographer's Guide to the Big Island: Being in the Right Place, at the Right Time, for the Best Image! is the book for you.**

# Introduction

## This Book Is For *YOU!*

Most people come to the Big Island with less time than they would like. WITH SO MANY POSSIBILITIES AND OPTIONS, many find themselves unable to easily locate and photograph the magnificent places they would like to capture while visiting here.

Whether you are only here for only a couple of days, or have the luxury of a longer stay - *this guidebook will prove to be invaluable, as it shares the best and most dynamic locations to capture images on the Big Island and how to easily access them.*

*This book will save you precious time and effort.*

*You don't have to scout out and discover the best locations and you don't have to wonder if you missed any of the great or spectacular places.*

**Rather you can casually move from one marvelous site to another, with clear expectations and relaxed certainty, given the amount of time you do have available.**

To be sure, scouting out and discovering the best places for the best image are part of the fun of creative photography, *but if you are short on time, why not put the odds in your favor?*

Welcome to Hawai'i Island, known as the Big Island! May you enjoy, appreciate, and capture its great wonder and beauty.

# Let the Adventure Begin…

For the ease of finding the most photogenic locations on the Big Island – let us begin in Kona, where the vast majority of people arrive on the island.

The Highway system on the Big Island is very simplistic. Highway 19 runs both north and south from Kona airport, and is found with great ease.

**We will begin by going directly north from Kona and circling the island - returning back to Kona, with a number of impressive side routes along the way. The sites will be most easily found by locating the specific highway mile markers for each photo op. The distance and time from Kona and/or Hilo is also included.**

Many of the sites can be visited in one day. Then it's just a matter of lighting, as to how successful the outcome of your images will be. In some cases, sunrise and sunset lighting will make the image more dynamic, in other cases sunrise and sunset lighting are not a particularly strong factor for a successful image.

*To help you best optimize your time - for every location shared, a "**best time to be there**" paragraph, or two is included.*

Certainly follow your heart and give yourself permission to have the best experience possible. And if you focus on quality over quantity you will allow yourself the opportunity to capture a higher percent of dynamic, if not extraordinary images.

Most locations are within easy walking distance from the car, with safe, easy access.

A few sites will require more effort, such as hiking, as they are more remote. In a few cases, a 4-wheel drive vehicle would be ideal. If you do not have access to one - most locations will be within walking distance.

However long you may visit the Big Island, whether for a couple of days or over several weeks, drink deeply of its beauty, its wonder, and magnificence, ***and*** allow yourself to bask fully in the Spirit of Aloha!

## A Quick Word ...
## About What to Bring & Safety

While visiting these excellent photo locations, for your over all convenience, it is often best to have a hat, for either sun or rain, and have sunscreen, just in case, because the sun can be intense in places. Sunglasses are optional and regarding footwear, sandals or slippa's as they are called here, work well at most places.

However, be aware, it may be best to protect your feet (from lava - scratches and cuts) by wearing comfortable walking/hiking shoes.

Food and water are available in most areas around the island, *but it is wise* to carry food or snacks and always have water with you, in case you stay out shooting late and the restaurants are closed by the time you return.

Shorts and a t-shirt or a light blouse are often the norm for daylight hours. The weather, however, is unpredictable and can change at any given moment and often does. So it is best to carry layers with you and be prepared.

If you go to Hawai'i Volcanoes National Park, it can be quite cool there in the evenings. Thanks to its higher elevation – 4000 ft. and the windward (rainier) location of the park, it is always cooler than most of the island. At least in the upper elevations of the park, so it best to bring a sweater or light jacket. Moreover, it's always wise to have rain gear and a fleece on hand, especially in winter.

## Safety Tips!

Commons sense is the key word for having a safe and pleasurable visit while on the Big Island.

Drink plenty of water, so as to not get dehydrated, wearing clothing and footwear appropriate to your location, and being aware of that unsuspecting rouge wave that comes along every so often, will be a big step towards assuring an incident free visit.

Also the Big Island has no four lane freeways, only two lane highways and the top speed limit is still only 55 m.p.h. - so be aware and be alert - while driving the islands highways and roadways.

**Remember always, Safety First!**

## Expect the Unexpected...
## Enhancing your Images Naturally!

The geographical location and positioning of the Big Island of Hawai'i affords more unexpected natural events, occurring more often, than on the US mainland.

Mists, rain, vog, (yes, even vog can be utilized to enhance an image) rainbows, cloud bursts, God rays, white rainbows, and moonbows (just like a rainbow, except at night, created around a full moon) are all abundant here.

Other natural occurrences that may be drawn upon to help create a more dynamic image include: the wind, the moon - in any phase. And of course, one hour before sun rise and sun set, as well as, one hour around either sun rise and sun set, also known as the "magic hour."

While the daily events in the third paragraph can be more or less calculated into creating your images, the natural events in the second paragraph can appear unexpectedly and at any moment. They may last from a few seconds to several minutes.

The aware photographer *is* always on the look out for such occurrences, to be included in their images, thus capturing a more dynamic image, and mixed with a little imagination – creating a thrilling and satisfying extraordinary image.

# Ready, Camera, Action...

One of the best places for capturing sunset images on the west side of the island is known locally as Kua Bay. The state has given it the name of Manini'owli Beach, and it is a part of the Kekaha Kai State Park.

Of course, any beach with a sunset setting available, has the potential for a fabulous sunset image. But for some reason, Kua Bay continually presents extraordinary image potentials. As it turns out, it is my personal favorite location for capturing sunsets.

***The best time to be there:*** *Because this excellent beach is so close to Kona, it is very crowded and busy during the day, so the best time to be there is from about 45 mins. before sunset to half an hour after sunset.*

Towards sunset, the crowds begin to disappear rapidly, leaving more places to choose from to plant your tripod. The reflection in the water after the sunset is often spectacular as well, so don't leave too soon. The only limiting factor is that the park closes at 7 pm and they do lock the gates, so you need be out by then.

**To get there:** Get on Highway 19 heading north from Kona. You will pass the Kona airport, continue on until you reach mile marker 89. Once there, the turn off is the next *paved* road on the left, directly across the highway from the Veterans Cemetery. Make the turn and follow the road for over a mile, until you meet the cul-de-sac where the restrooms are. Park and walk the paved pathway 1/4 block to the beach area.
Distance from Kona: 12 miles Time from Kona: 20 mins.

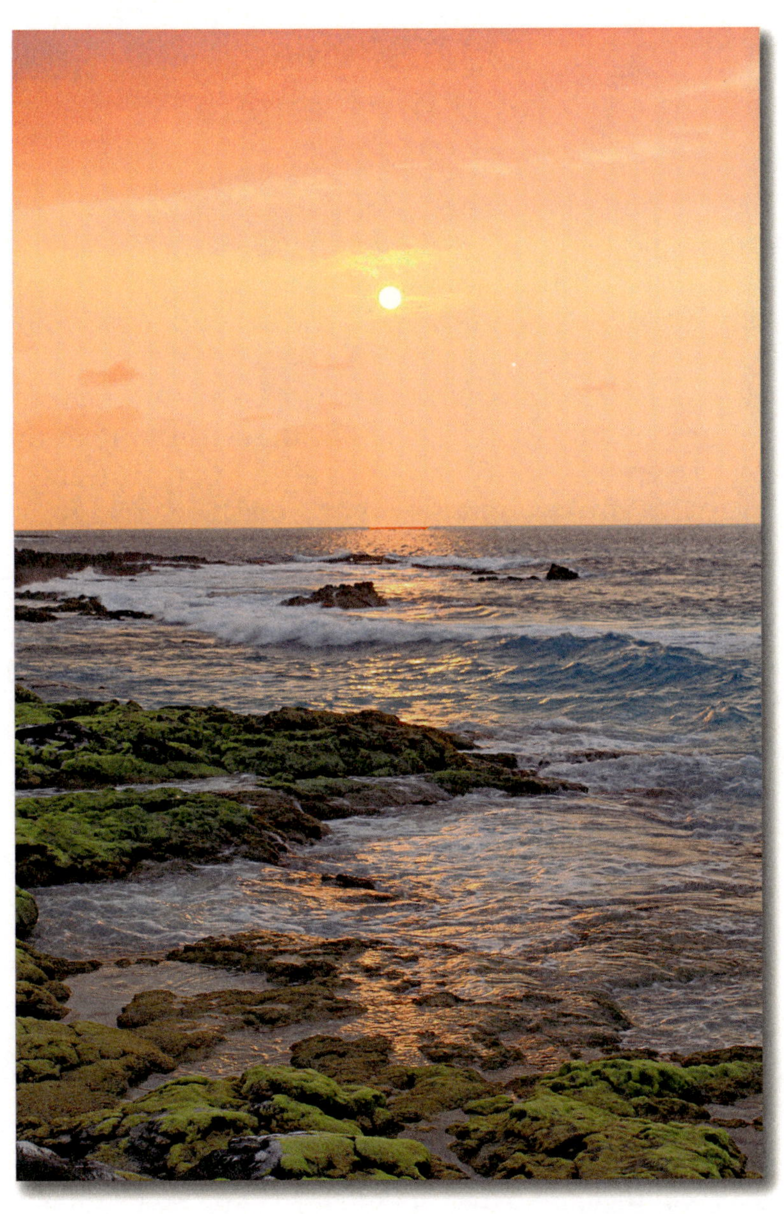

Sunset, Kua Bay 1

# A Quick Note...
# about the Camera

This is a guidebook specifically designed to share with you – where to potentially be in the right place, at the right time, for the best image. It is not a book specifically about the techniques, or the art of photography.

It would be amiss, however, not to mention a few camera details with the insight **that could mean the difference between being able to capture an extraordinary image - over a ordinary image!**

***I feel it important enough to bring this to your attention before proceeding any further...***
as there are ways to adjust the camera to "see" more like the eye sees. Ways to adjust the camera settings that allow you to capture a truer rendition of the scene before you - regarding both the light and color available.

If you do not make any adjustments in your camera, then you will always get the same kind of image. Most often - falling short of the full volume of color and light.

In order, not to disrupt the flow of getting you to the best photo ops, the full "A Word about Your Camera" is on page 89.

***Again, I felt it important enough for you to be aware of the choices – toward creating the best images possible.***

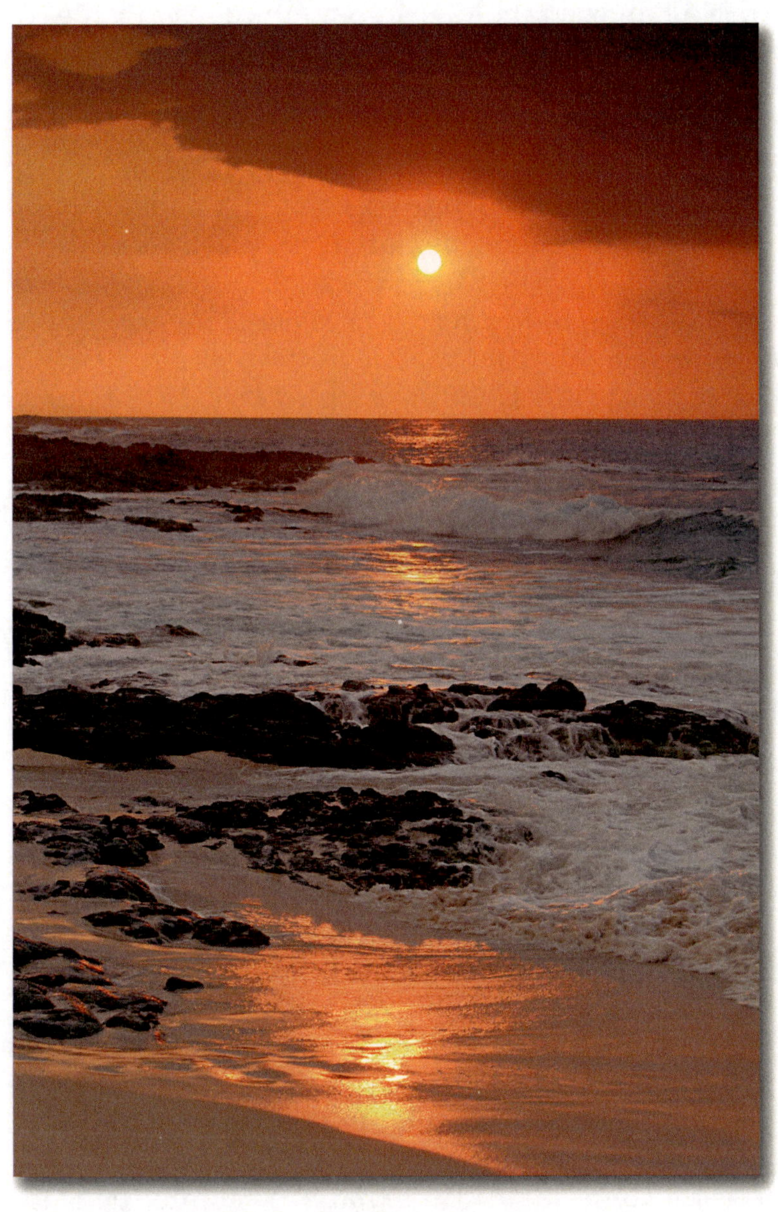

Sunset, Kua Bay 2

# Kiholo Bay

Kiholo Bay is a fabulous area, with indescribable blue water, abundant sea turtles, and refreshing cold water springs that bubble up and mix with the sea water.

This is a unique area, well worth the time and effort it takes to get there. It involves a bit of a hike, not strenuous, just often very warm.

***The best time to be there:*** *This is one of those places, that proves to be an excellent place to photograph any time of day. You could also try capturing a sunset here, but be sure and have a flash light for the walk back to your car.*

**To get there:** On Highway 19 heading north from Kona. continue on until you reach mile marker 82. Just south of mile marker 81 is a pull over area on the makai (ocean) side of the highway. At the pull out is a parking area (best to park on the highway.) From the parking area you will find a trail that becomes an old gravel road and heads straight down to the coast.

Stay on the trail/road and as you near the coast follow the signs that read "public access." Once on the sand, facing the ocean, turn right and follow the coastline to where it goes from sand to lava, just before a short wooden bridge.

Continue on the lava trail, in a couple of blocks distance you will see a small beach. You may also continue further by scrambling across the lava.

There are some small coves that project into the water of the bay. After the warm walk this is a great place to jump in the water for a cool refreshing dip.
You should see Hawaiian green sea turtles aplenty.

From Kona: 18 miles  Time from Kona: 25 - 30 mins.
Hike in time: 20 mins. each way. Be sure to have water!

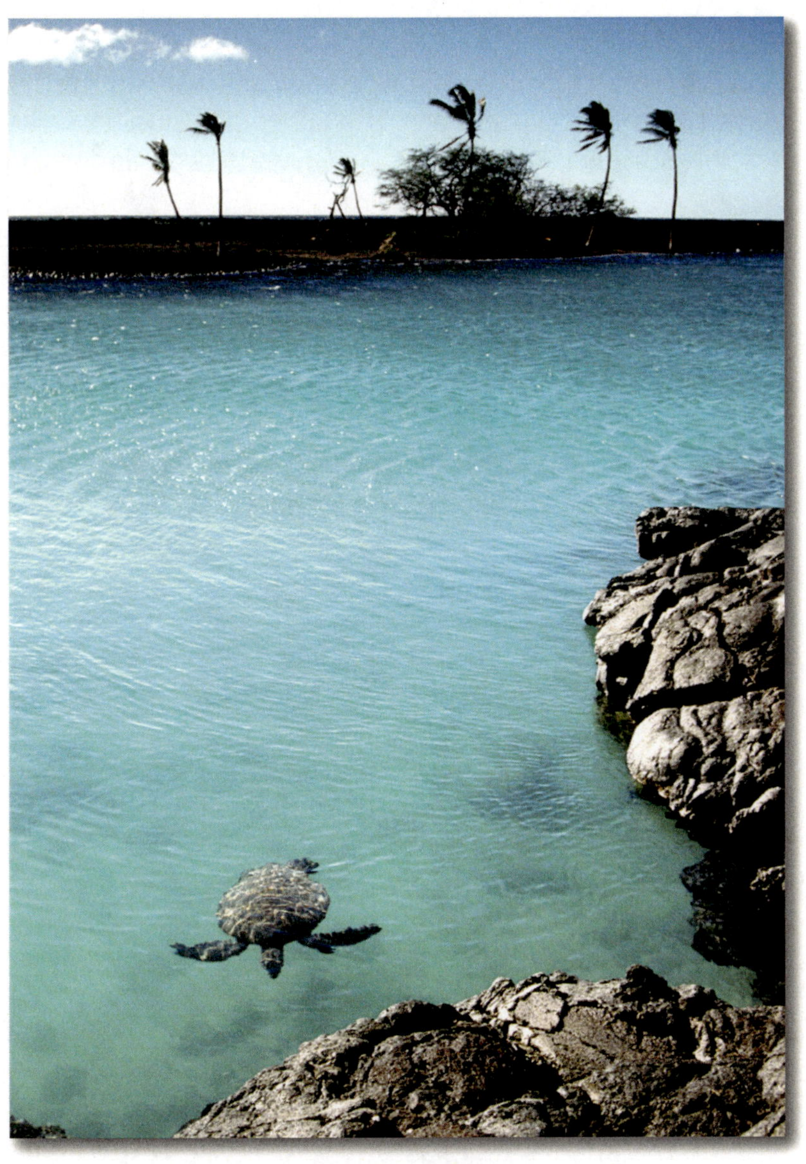

**Kiholo Bay**
**with Honu**
**(Hawaiian green sea turtle)**

# ‘Anaeho’omalu Bay
## (known locally as “A” Bay)

This is an exceptionally picturesque area. What makes it so are the many palm trees, the plumeria bushes/trees, (and sea turtles if you shoot directly at the oceans edge.)

The best images are captured on the resort side of the huge fishponds facing the ocean. When there is no wind, you can captured mirrored images, and when there is wind, the color reflections can be a sheer delight.

***The best time to be there:*** *About 45 mins. before sunset. This will give you time to scout a bit and see what's possible.*

**To get there:** Continuing north, to the Kona side of mile marker 76, there is a stoplight. It is the first stoplight you come to after the Kona airport. It is Waikoloa Beach Road and here you will turn left towards the ocean.

Just drive straight down Waikoloa Beach Road. You will soon come to a stop sign. There are the Queen Shops to your left. Continue straight another block to the second stop sign. Right after this stop sign there is a Shell gas station and the King Shops on your right.

Continue half a block further to the third stop sign. Here you will turn left. Stay on this road several blocks length and then it will “J” to the right into a big parking area. Park and continue walking on the road, right past the restrooms to the coastline. For those wanting to shoot the pond in the foreground, there is a path off to the right, just past the restrooms.
From Kona: 25 miles Time from Kona: about 35 mins.

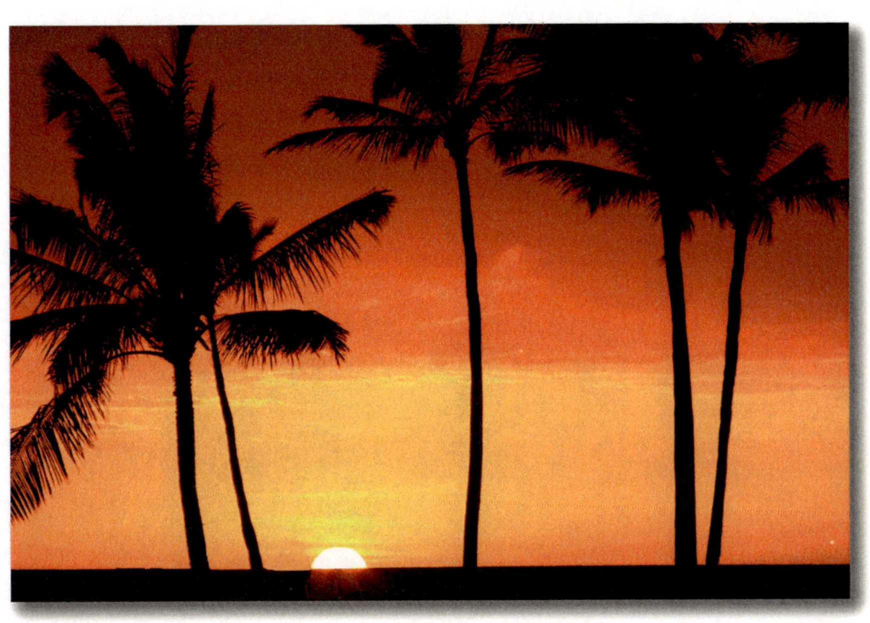

A Bay, Sunset 1

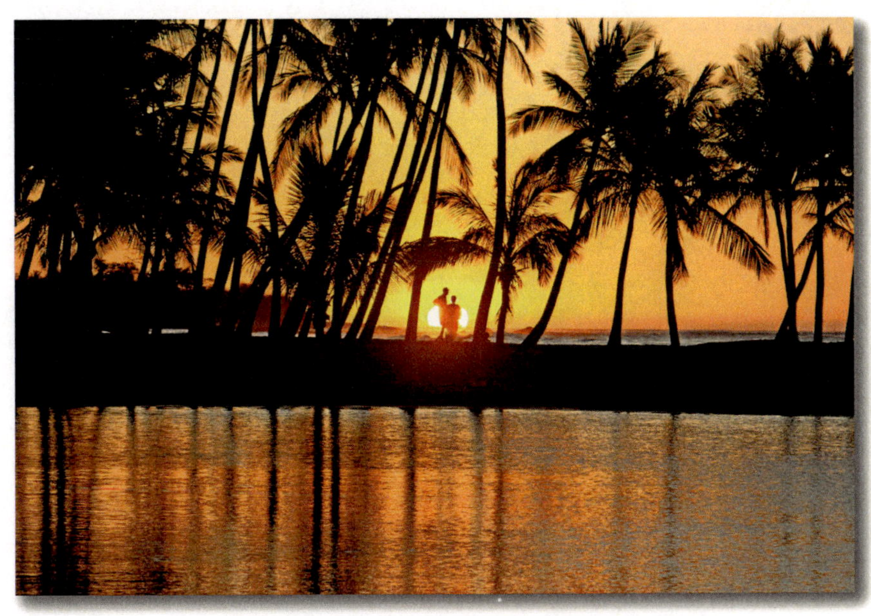

A Bay with Refection 1

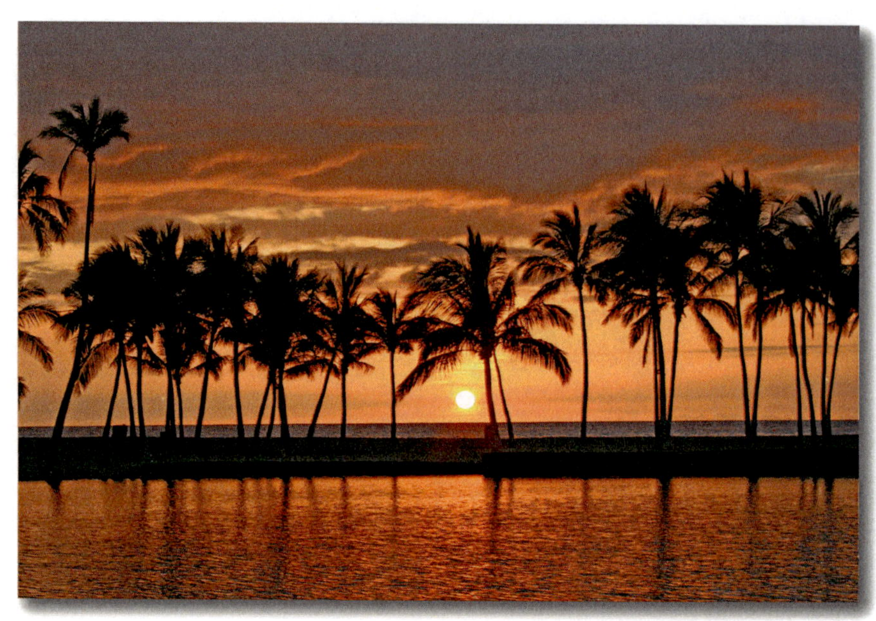

A Bay with Refection 2

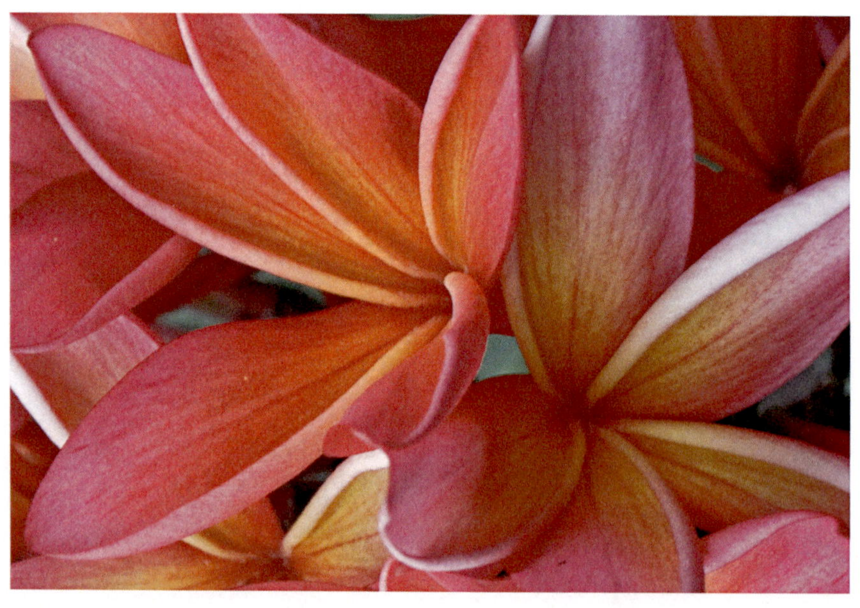

Plumeria Blossom at A Bay

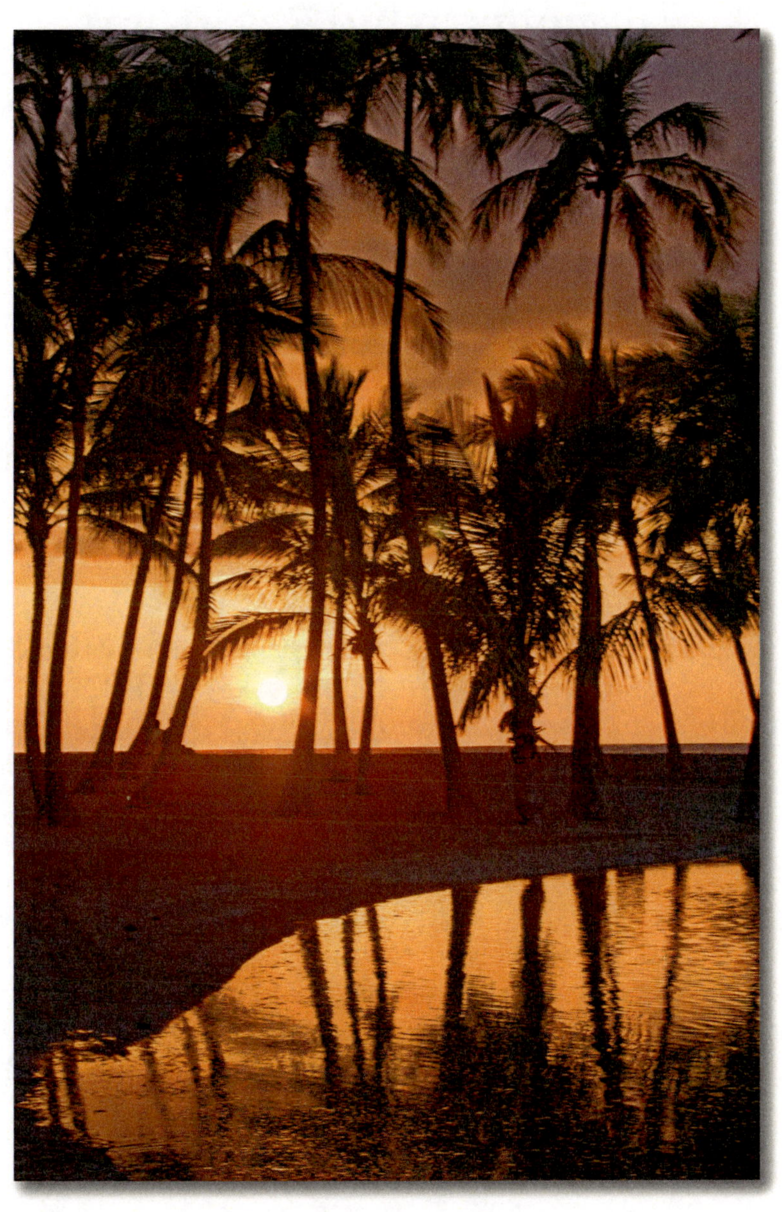

A Bay, Sunset 2

# Fairmont Orchid Resort area

One area that allows you to capture a *classic* Hawai'i image, is at the Fairmont Orchid Resort (see image 1.) It has a group of palm trees that are symmetrically, and when lined up with the setting sun and the sunset colors, can produce some very dynamic images. Often there are Hawaiian green sea turtles in the area that can be including in the image as well (see image 2.)

***The best time to be there:*** *About 45 mins. before sunset. This will give you time to scout a bit and see what's possible. Be sure to have your tripod placed and be ready to shoot* ***before*** *the sun gets too low. Get the sun in balanced alignment for a potential great image.*

**To get there:** Continuing north past Waikoloa Beach Road, to a half mile past mile marker 74, there is a stoplight. It is the second stoplight you come to after the Kona airport. It is Mani Lani Dr. and here you will turn left, towards the ocean.

Stay on Mani Lani Dr. about a mile to the round-about. You turn right at the round-about, and then go another mile to the resort. Look for a parking lot entrance on the left after you pass the resort sign. There is a fee to park that can be mitigated. Buy something at the deli, near the shore and show the receipt at the lobby desk upon departure.

Once parked, make your way to the lobby and beyond to the coastline. When you meet the sidewalk on the coastline, follow it to your left. You will see the palm trees. Take your time and explore towards the best possible image.

From Kona: 28 miles  Time from Kona: approx. 45 mins.

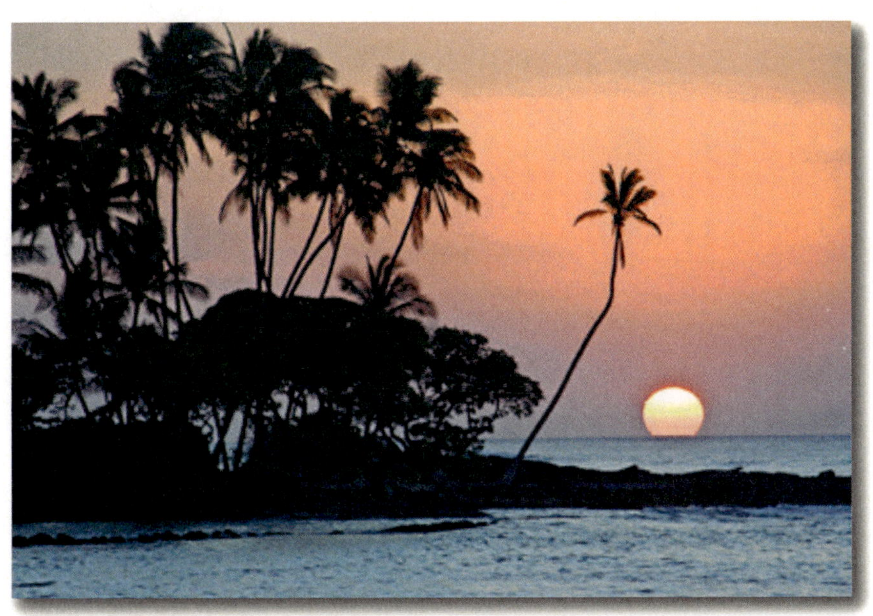

**Fairmont Orchid, Sunset** Image 1

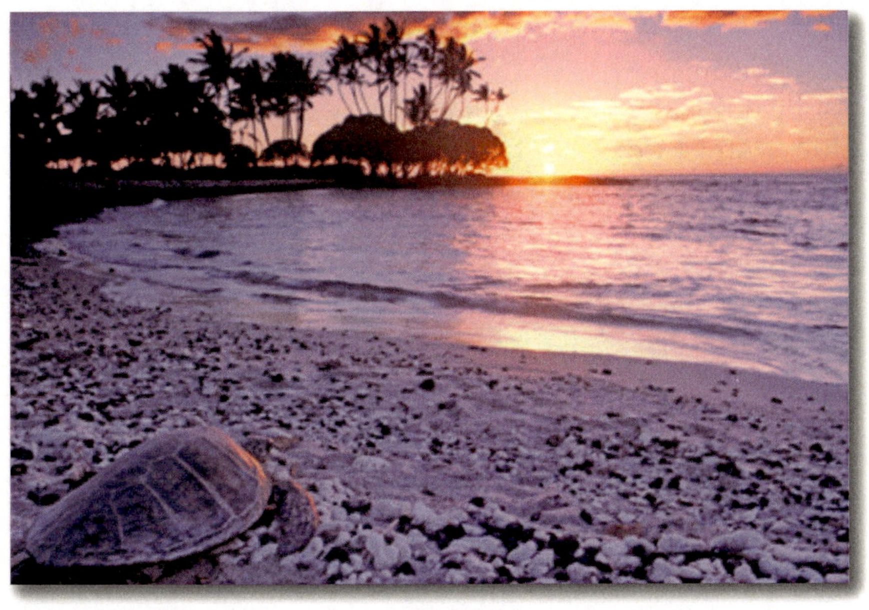

**Fairmont Orchid, Sunset** Image 2

# Kawaihae Cove

There is a little known area right near the Kawaihae Port. At least you won't see many photographers there. That's because it looks rather stark compared to other areas with more classic image potentials.

However, you can capture some great images here. You just have to line up the elements that are available... the setting sun, the sunset colors, the rocks the waves (if any) and the reflections, and/or you might just chance upon a magical sky (see image 2).

***The best time to be there:*** *About 25 mins. before sunset. There is not much to scout as it is a very small area. Best to be alert as to how the light is shifting as the sun actually sets and how this is impacting the image potential.*

**To get there:** From Kona, stay on Highway 19, heading north, till you come to a tee. This is after mile marker 68 or 32 miles north of Kona. Here you will turn left onto Highway 270. Go approximately 2 miles to the Kawaihae Port/Highway 270 junction. Highway 270 veers off to the right, **but you will continue straight to the harbor area**.

It couldn't be easier to find. From the junction continue on about an 1/8 of a mile. The road ends at the harbor, with plenty of places to park. Once parked, simple walk to the end of the road, around the barrier, and onto the sand. This is exactly where you want to be for that sunset shot. Just before you reach the cove you will see the Kawaihae Club outrigger canoes on the right and by the way, Café Pesto - a couple blocks back is a great place to eat.
From Kona: 35 miles Time from Kona: approx. 45 mins.

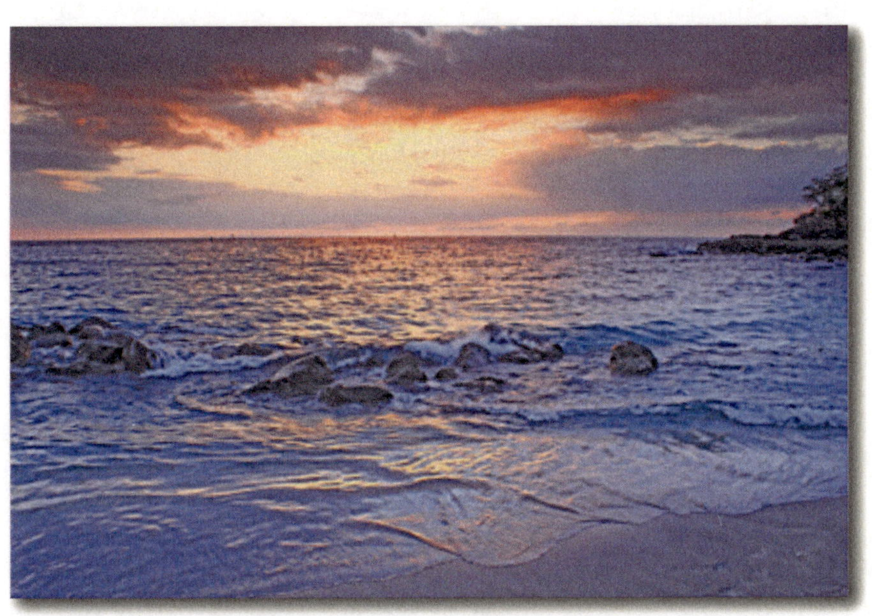

**Kawaihae Reflections**

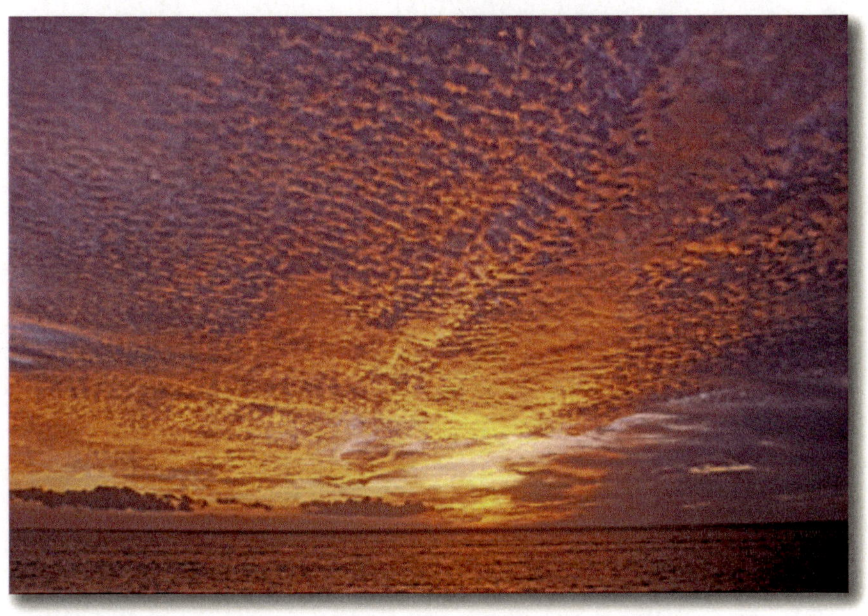

**Kawaihae Magic Sunset** Image 2

# Pololu Valley Overlook

Pololu Valley Overlook is one of the most outstanding viewpoints on the island, along with the upcoming Waipio Overlook. You will find it at the very end of highway 270.

This viewpoint at 400 ft. elevation offers a unique perspective of the rugged raw beauty of the Big Island, a fabulous coastline, and a black sand beach.

You may opt to hike down into Pololu Valley and spend some in the magnificence of the black sand beach.

***The best time to be there:*** *Any time of day is a great time to be there. If you try at dawn you might be lucky and get cloud colored reflections. The same goes for sunset as well, but some of the best images created can be throughout the day - all according to the play of lighting and clouds.*

**To get there:** From Kona, stay on Highway 19, heading north, till you come to a tee. This is after mile marker 68 or 32 miles north of Kona. Here you will turn left onto highway 270 (reset your milage gauge at the tee.)

Go approximately 2 miles to the Kawaihae Port/highway 270 junction. Highway 270 veers off to the right at the junction, **be sure to veer right and stay on highway 270**.

Simply continue on highway 270 for 28 miles from the tee, to where the road ends at small parking area. Take your time here to find the best image possibilities. You can also capture some excellent images part way down the trail, as well as on the beach.
From Kona: 61 miles Time from Kona: approx. 90 mins.

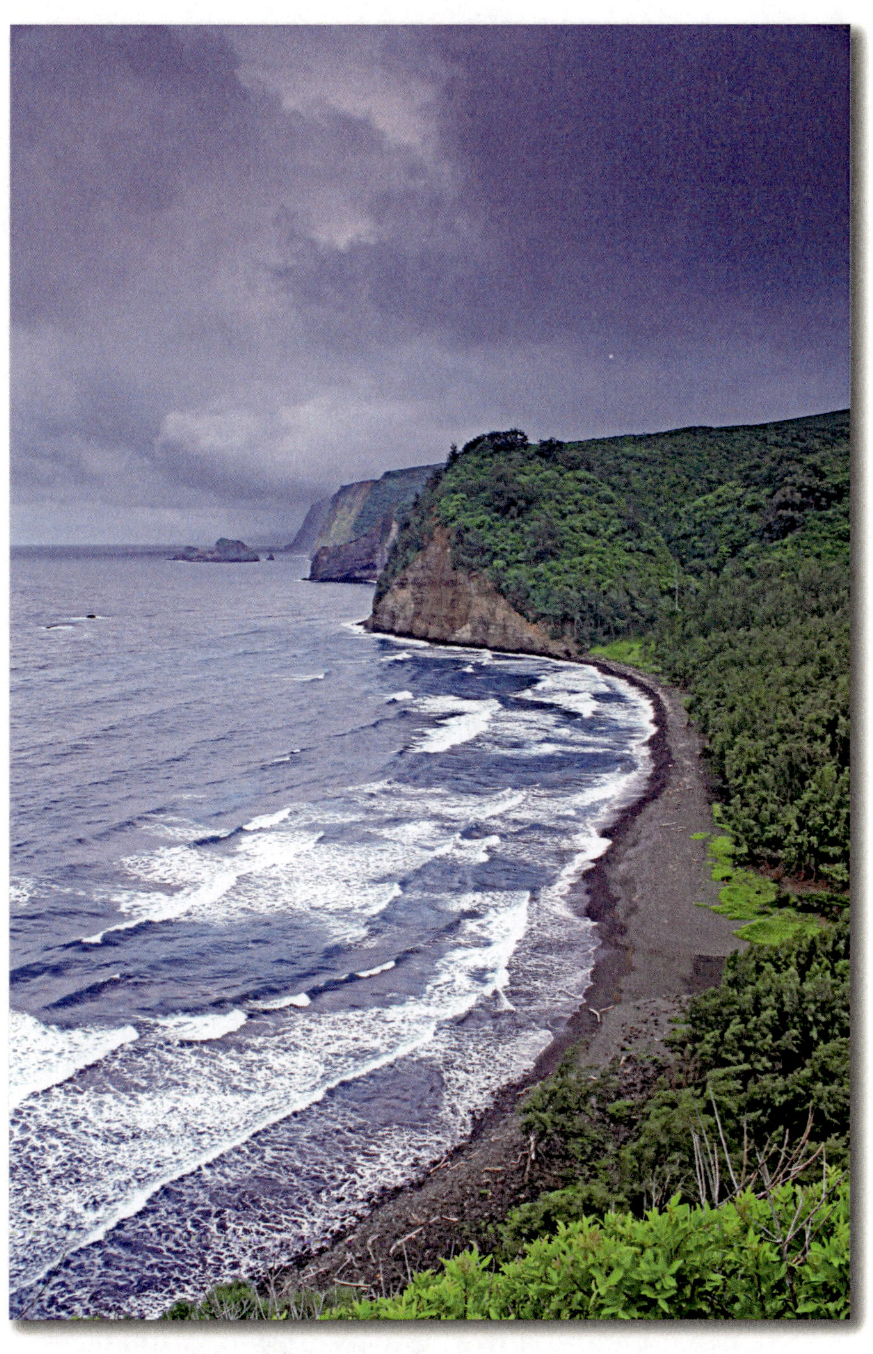

**Image from Pololu Valley Overlook**

# Waipio Valley Overlook

Be prepared for another astonishing vista. The Waipio Valley Overlook, along with the Pololu Valley Overlook both offer awesome image potential captures.

The Waipio Valley Overlook at several 100 ft. above sea level, is one of the nicest views you will find on the Big Island. If you have a 4-wheel drive, or you are an avid hiker you may opt to visit Waipio Valley and/or Waipio black sand Beach. You will find further astonishing photo ops here.

***The best time to be there:*** *Any time of day is a great time to be there. If you try at dawn you might be lucky and capture the bluff lit up by the first rays of sun. You can also capture cloud colored reflections as well. The same goes for evening regarding cloud colored reflections. Some of the best images are created throughout the day… depending on the play of lighting and clouds.*

**To get there: From the Pololu Valley Overlook**
Leave the overlook area returning the way you came until you reach mile marker 21. At mile marker 21, you will turn left (uphill) onto highway 250.

*This is a very scenic route, and well worth the drive, it will take you to higher elevations, with wonderful views, green rolling hills, and potential rainbows.*

Climb uphill approx. 2 miles until you reach a stop sign. Turn right at the stop sign and stay on highway 250 for a little over 17 miles until it meets up with highway 19. Turn left and follow highway 19 into Waimea.

* ***In Waimea you will come to a stoplight. You will turn***

*left at the stoplight and continue on Highway 19 for another 13.5 miles until you reach a signed left hand turn for Waipio Valley.*

*Once you turn, you will drop down a mile or so, until you come to a stop sign. Turn left here (you are now on highway 240) and follow the highway out another 8 miles until it ends at the Waipio Valley Overlook parking area.*

From Pololu Valley Overlook: 59 miles Time from Pololu Valley Overlook: approx. 1 hr. 30 mins.

**To get there: From the Kawaihae Harbor**

From the Kawaihae Harbor, head back to the Kawaihae/ Kona junction (approx.. 2 miles.) When you reach the junction, stay on Highway 19, going straight (uphill). *Do not turn right at the junction going back towards Kona.*

Continue uphill for 8 miles. Here you will reach the highway 250 junction, and in another two miles you will reach the stoplight in Waimea mentioned above (see paragraph with asterisk and italicized sentences above) to get you the rest of the way to the Waipio Valley Overlook parking area.

From the Kawaihae Harbor: 33 miles
Time from the Kawaihae Harbor: approx. 50 mins.

**To get there: Directly from Kona**

Go to Palani St. on highway 19, at mile marker 100 in Kona. Turn uphill. This is the beginning of highway 190, and it will take you most directly to Waimea.

Stay on highway 190 until you reach the first stoplight in Waimea. At the light continue straight on highway 19 (see paragraph with asterisk and italicized sentences above) to get you the rest of the way to the Waipio Valley Overlook parking area.
From Kona: 63 miles Time from Kona: approx. 1hr. 25 mins.

***Please be Aware…*** that Palani St. is also where highway 19 and highway 11 meet. The 100 mile marker is the beginning of Highway 19 heading north.

If you go south from Palani St., you will be on highway 11. It's the same road just with different starting and/or ending point for each highway.

If you go south from Palani St., you will be on highway 11 and the next mile marker will read mm 122 and diminish every mile until you reach Hilo.

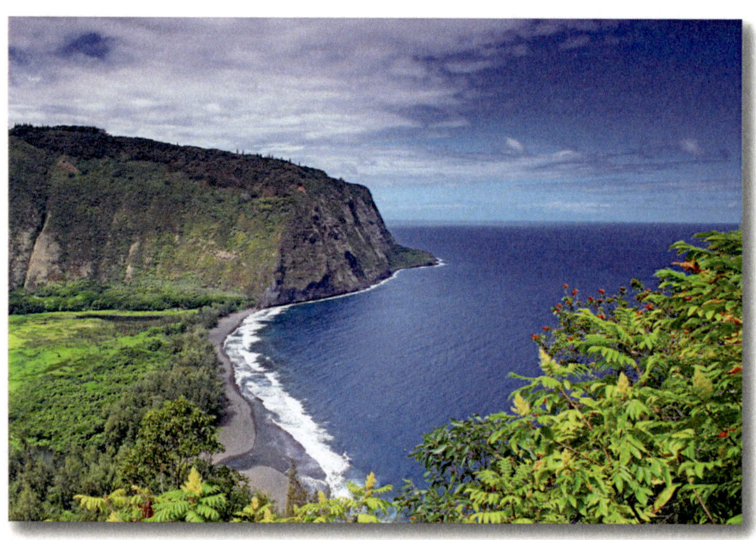

**Image from Waipio Valley Overlook area**

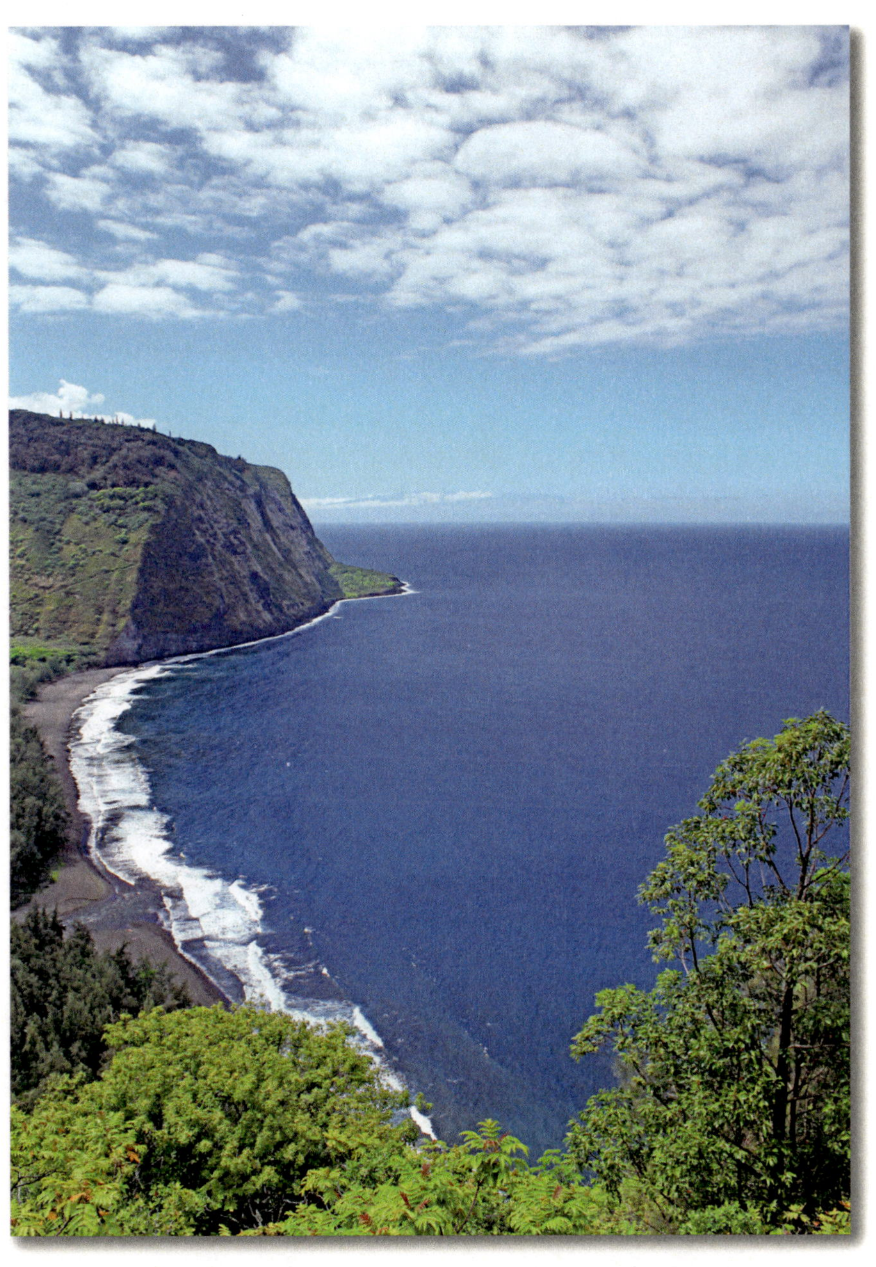

From Waipio Valley Overlook

# Waterfalls on the Hamakua Coast

You may have noticed that once you reached a certain point on your way to the Pololu Valley Overlook, things all of a sudden changed color and began to look green.

The hillsides were green instead of dry, the landscape became filled with more abundant flora and fauna, there were even a few creeks with running water that you crossed over.

This is because you crossed into the "wet" side of the island, (the north and eastside) where the rainfall is abundant – up to 240 inches a year, compared to the west (Kona) side where the average rainfall is 8 -14 inches a year.

Once you climb to the higher elevation points on your way to Waimea, again the landscape becomes wonderfully green, and generally stays that way through Waimea and down to Waipio, and also along the Hamakua Coast.

The Hamakua Coast is where we are now about to venture, to some of the most beautiful waterfalls on the island, if not the entire state.

There are a multitude of waterfalls on this side of the island, most are difficult to access. Lucky for us, there are 3 excellent and easily accessible waterfalls.

They are by name, Kama'e'e Falls, Akaka Falls, and Rainbow Falls, plus a few others along the way.

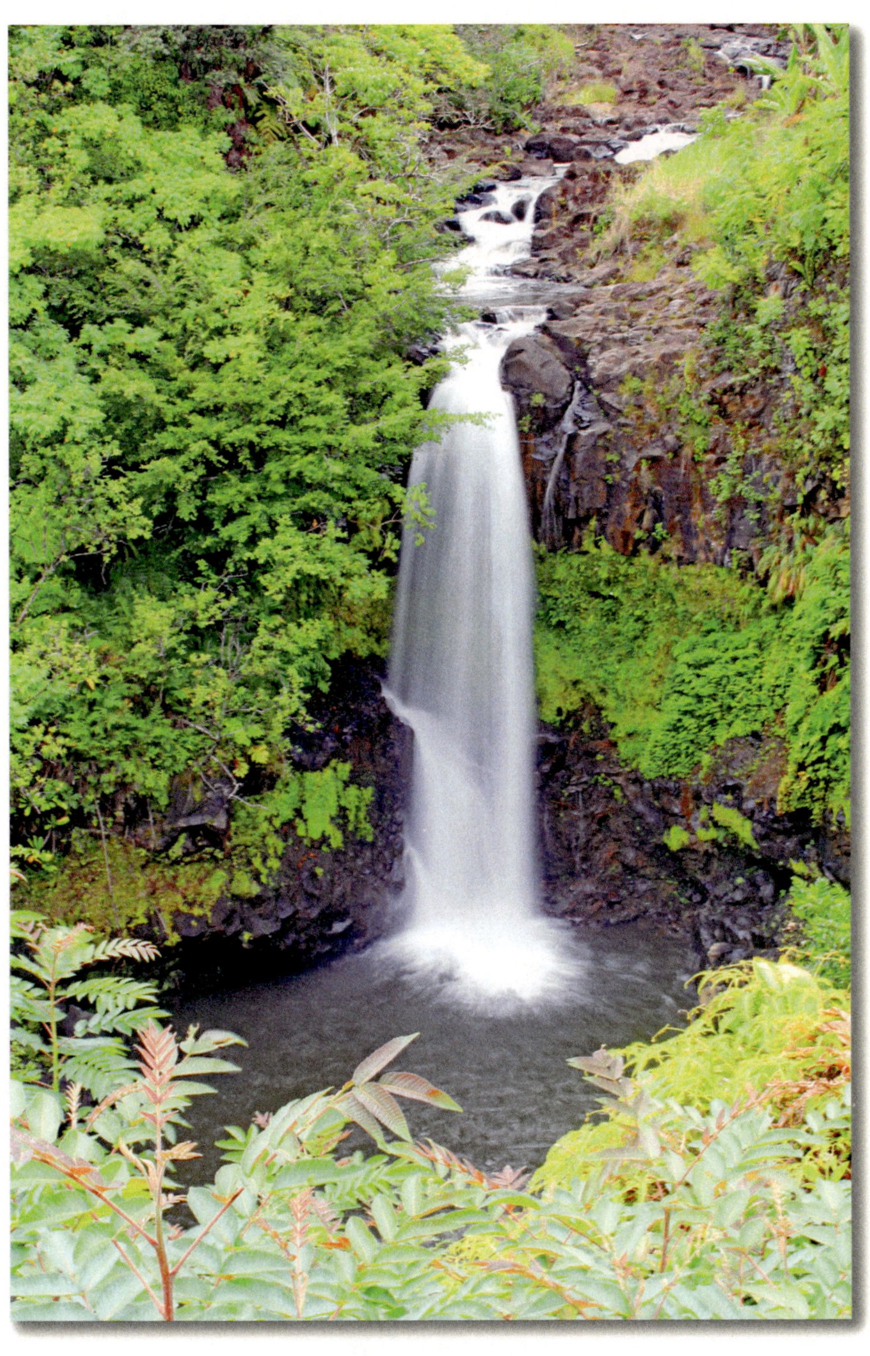

Kama'e'e Falls

# Kama'e'e Falls

Kama'e'e Falls is a charming, little-known, seldom visited waterfall. It sits on private land with public access. Its location is a couple of miles off highway 19.

While Akaka Falls and Rainbow Falls are much higher and fuller falls, and are certainly more widely known, Kama'e'e Falls has a more graceful and gentle quality.

***The best time to be there:*** *If you want to shoot the falls with the sun directly on the waterfall it is best to be there before 2 pm. If you want to get a silky effect to your image, then it will be best to wait until the waterfall is in shadow, which is after 2 pm depending on the time of year.*

**To get there: From Waipi'o Valley Overlook**

Be sure to visit **Waipio Valley Artworks** before leaving the area. Turn left on Kukuihale Rd., 1 block from the overlook. Continue about 3 blocks. It's on the left. It has great local art and wonderful snacks.

Head away from the Waipi'o Valley Overlook and back onto highway 250, continuing **straight through** the little town of Honoka'a (half a block down on the right hand side, after the first stop sign you reach in Honoka'a, is a great gift shop called **Taro Patch**. Stop in and say aloha to Edie the owner!)

Once you reach the far side of Honoka'a, you will come to a stop sign and a tee. This is Highway 19 near mile marker 42. Turn left onto highway 19 and continue on until you reach mile marker 16 area.

*** Shortly before mm 16, there is a unnamed falls you**

**can see it from the highway, on the right hand side, as you cross a bridge. You can stop and shoot an image of this waterfall, but be sure to pull over in a safe place, completely off the highway. Be careful & safe as you make your way to capture this falls.**

**Shortly after the bridge you will see a sign for the World Botanical Garden with a zip line. Turn right at the next road. The name of this road is Leopolino.**

**After a short block it tees. At the tee, turn right again and go about a block, to the first road on the left. Turn left and continue up this mostly single lane road for approx. 2 miles. Look for a gravel road on the left and turn onto the road and through a gate. It has a small Kama'e'e Falls sign next to the gate.**

**Continue on the gravel road for a short half mile. It will turn right, climb a bit, turn left and there you are in a gravel parking lot. Once out of the car you will hear the falls, walk straight towards the fence with the wooden top in front of you.**
From Waipio: 39 miles Time from Waipio: approx. 50 mins.

**To get there: Directly from Kona**

Go to Palani St. on highway 19, at mile marker 100 in Kona. Turn uphill. This is the beginning of highway 190, and it will take you most directly to Waimea. Stay on highway 190 until you reach the first stoplight in Waimea. At the light **continue straight** on highway 19 through Waimea and downhill 15 miles skirting the town of Honoka'a. Continue on to the mm 16 area (see paragraph with asterisk and italicized sentences above) to get you the rest of the way to the Kama'e'e Falls. From Kona: 83 miles Time from Kona: approx. 95 mins.

# Akaka Falls

Akaka Falls is a unique tropical sanctuary unto itself – one of great natural beauty mixed with wild nature, multicolored plants, and colossal trees. Even though you are walking on a paved path, you feel as though you are walking in a very exotic and remote location.

There are giant bamboo, banana plants, wild orchids, and enormous trees with vines wrapped around them like a scene out of Jurassic Park. There are two large waterfalls, Akaka and Kahuna Falls, and two smaller ones with gentle flowing streams.

When you get to the Akaka Falls viewpoint, you are treated to an amazing vista – a 440 ft. waterfall surrounded by multihued greens of draping ferns, vines, and various indigenous trees.

In fact, it was recently voted the most favorite waterfall in all of Hawai'i, therefore, making it the most well known and most popular waterfall in the entire state. And rightly so, it is beautiful and majestic, and is a *great* photo op for a classic Hawai'i waterfall image.

While most people just stop by for a quick photo, take the time to walk more of the trail and explore the area. This is a nice option if you're looking for a little more quiet time and a deeper experience.

***The best time to be there:*** *Is between 9 am and 1 pm, if you want sunlight directly on the waterfall. Before 9am and after 1pm if you want to catch it without direct sunlight, either way will allow you to capture a great image.*

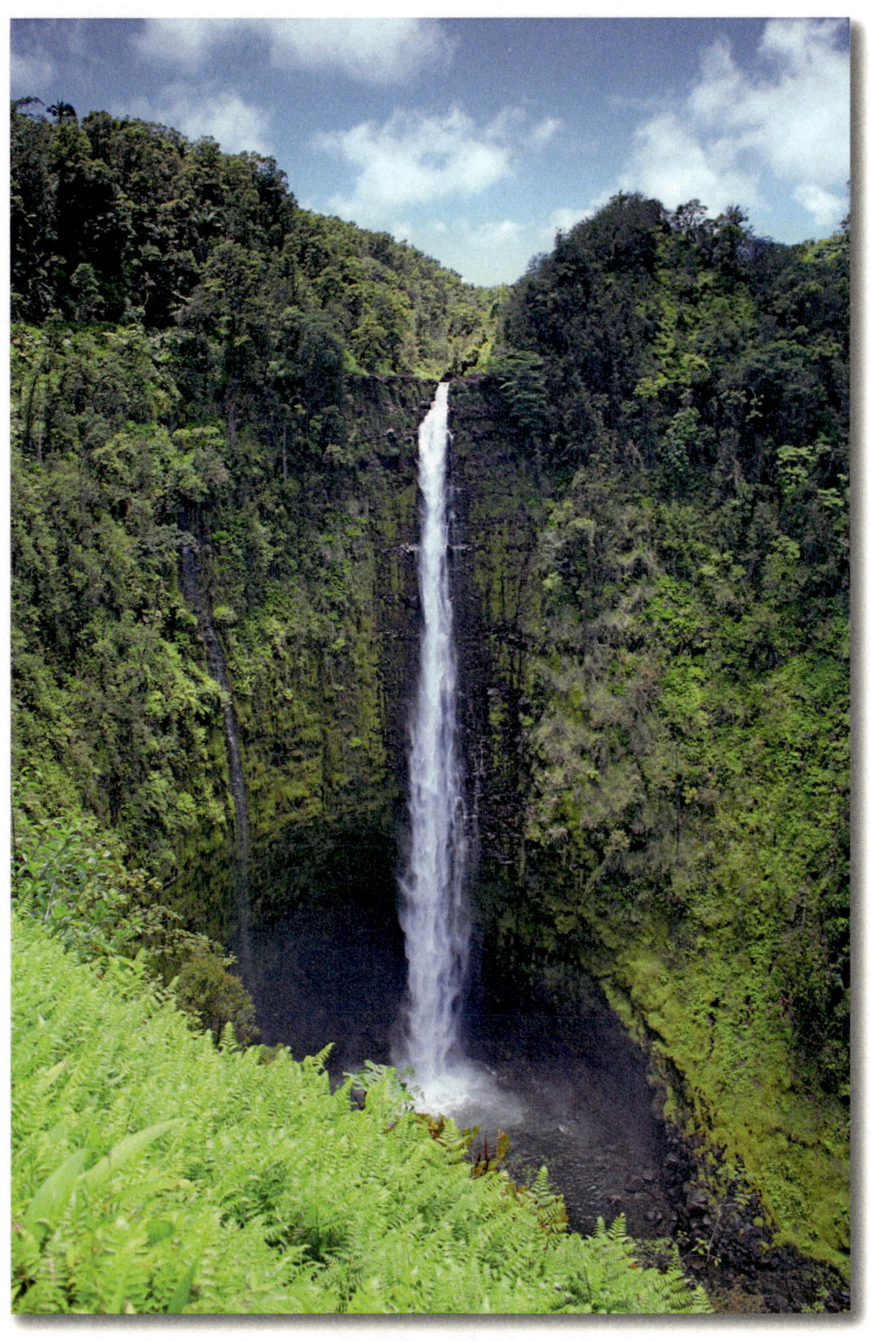

# Akaka Falls

### To get there: From Kama'e'e Falls

Turn around and head back to highway 19. Turn right at the highway and go past mile marker 14. Turn right onto highway 220 and follow the directions below in bold.

From Kama'e'e Falls: approx. 8.5 miles Time from Kama'e'e Falls: approx. 20 mins.

### To get there: From Kona

Akaka Falls State Park is less than half an hour from downtown Hilo, and about two hours from Kona. **To get there, turn off of Highway 19 onto Highway 220 between mile markers 13 and 14 near the town of Honomu.**

**The three and a half mile road to Akaka Falls passes through Honomu (a great place to get a sandwich, something to drink, and visit the craft shops, and a gallery. Especially give the Woodshop Gallery Cafe a try.**

**The road after Honomu continues uphill through old sugar plantations and eventually dead ends at the small parking lot – that fills up quickly.**

**A lot of visitors park on the road just before, and outside, the parking lot. Admission to Akaka Falls State Park is $1 per person, if you park outside the parking lot. Or $5 per car, plus $1 per person if you park in the parking lot. Park visiting hours:**

**6 am – 6 pm**

From Kona: 86 miles Time from Kona : approx. 2 hours.

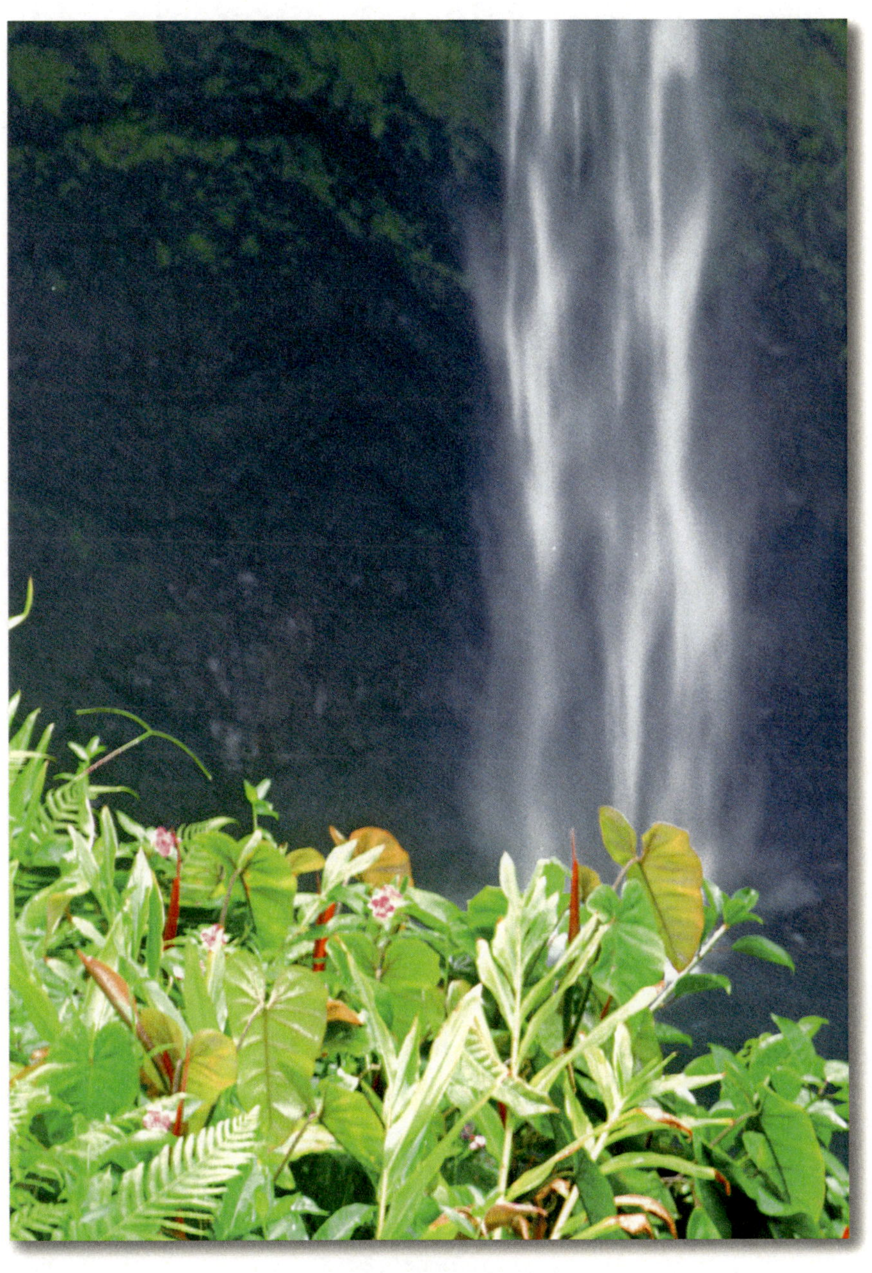

**Akaka Falls 2**

# Onomea Falls at the Hawai'i Tropical Botanical Gardens

Onomea Falls is a beautiful multi-tiered waterfall within the Hawai'i Tropical Botanical Gardens. If you are a waterfall enthusiast, then you will definitely want to include a stop here to capture these incredible falls.

There are over 2,500 exotic marked plants and astonishing array of tropical flowers (for all you flower aficionados out there) and an incredible view of Onomea Bay. There is the $15.00 per person entry fee, but really, for all that you will see (and can photograph) it's well worth it, plus you are supporting their efforts towards preservation and education.

***The best time to be there:*** *They open at 9 am and close at 5 pm with 4 pm being the latest you can enter. With the falls being among many trees, there is often a mix of light and shade on the water. Usually between 12 noon and 3 pm is the best time to capture these wondrous falls.*

**To get there: From Kona**

Follow highway 190 to Waimea, stay highway 19 to the Hamakua Coast until you pass the 8 mile marker. Look for the blinking yellow light with sign on the right saying "Old Mamalahoa Hwy." Make the next left onto the Scenic Route. About 1.5 miles on the left is the Hawai'i Tropical Botanical Gardens Visitor Center. From Kona: 90 miles Time from Kona : approx. 2 hours.

The Garden is located about 7 miles north of Hilo. Take Route 19 north. Just after mile marker 7, turn right at the large blue highway sign on the right saying "Scenic Route." About 1.5 miles on the left is the Visitor Center.

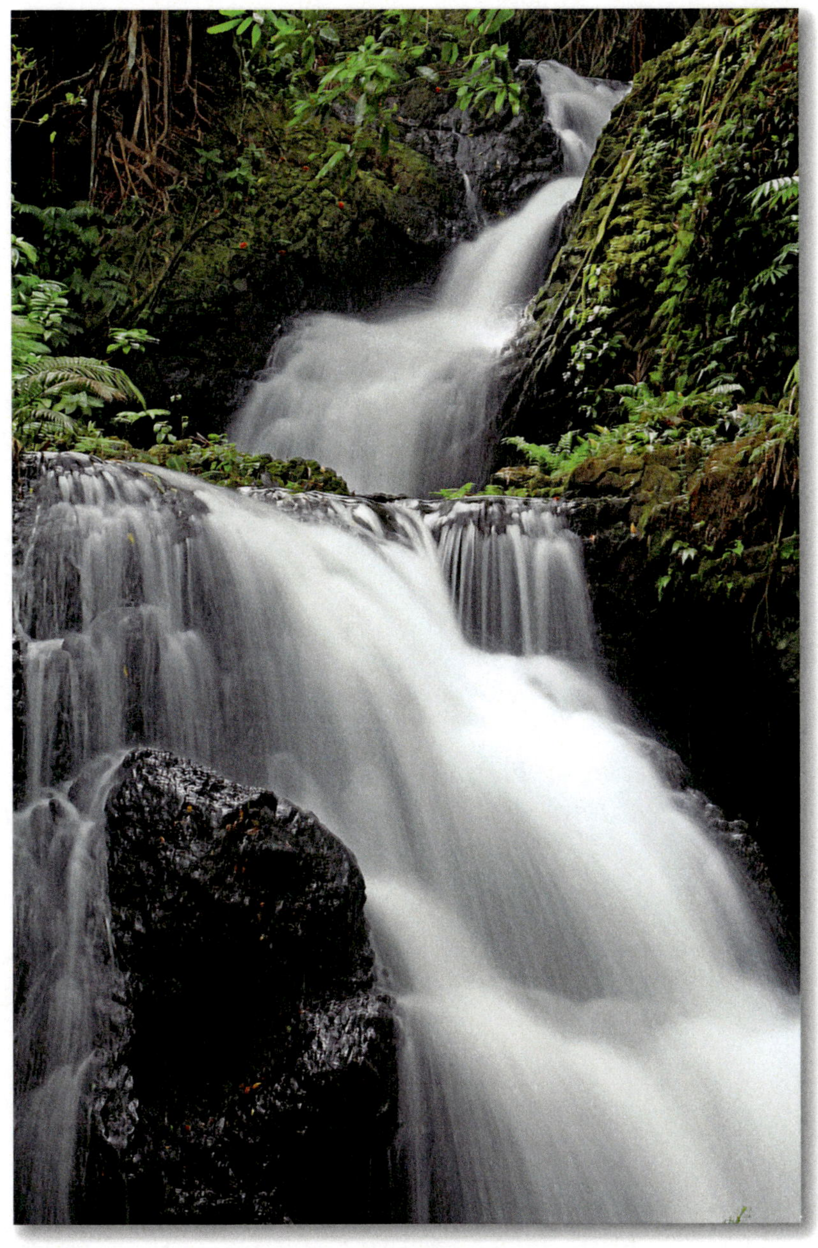

**Onomea Falls**

# Rainbow Falls

On the northern edge of scenic Hilo town, the gorgeous Waianuenue, commonly known as Rainbow Falls, flows and cascades 100 ft. into a picturesque refreshing pool.

The Hawaiian name Waianuenue, quite literally means "rainbow seen in water," and gets its name from the colorful rainbows that can often be seen in the swirling mist that rises from the river in the early morning light.

The foliage around the basin of the falls is lush, and tropical. It includes mango trees covered with philodendron, African tulip trees, kukui trees (candlenut - the Hawaiian state tree), banana trees and a variety of tropical flowers.

When the rains are heavy, it is an unleashed torrent of raging water. On most days it is an oasis of beauty and serenity

***The best time to be there:*** *Although Rainbow Falls is beautiful at all times, be sure to get there early in the morning before the tour buses arrive.*

*This is also the best time to see the rainbows in the waterfall mists. If you time it right, you could have the falls all to yourself. This is the best way to have the deepest experience while there.*

**To get there: From Kona**

Follow highway 190 to Waimea, stay on highway 19 along the Hamakua Coast until you pass the 3 mile marker in Hilo, turn mauka (inland, toward the mountain) on Waianuenue Avenue. As you drive up Waianuenue Avenue, you will pass the Hilo Public library on your right and soon Hilo High School also on your right.

After you pass the high school, get into the farthest right lane. You will pass through a traffic light intersection. After you pass through the traffic light, the road will start to curve.

Get into the lane farthest to the right. You will pass a baseball park on your right called Carvaleo park. You will now notice signs leading you to the falls. Take a right onto Rainbow Drive. Drive up a couple of blocks and the parking lot to the falls will be to your right.
From Kona: 95 miles  Time from Kona : approx. 2 hrs. 15 minutes

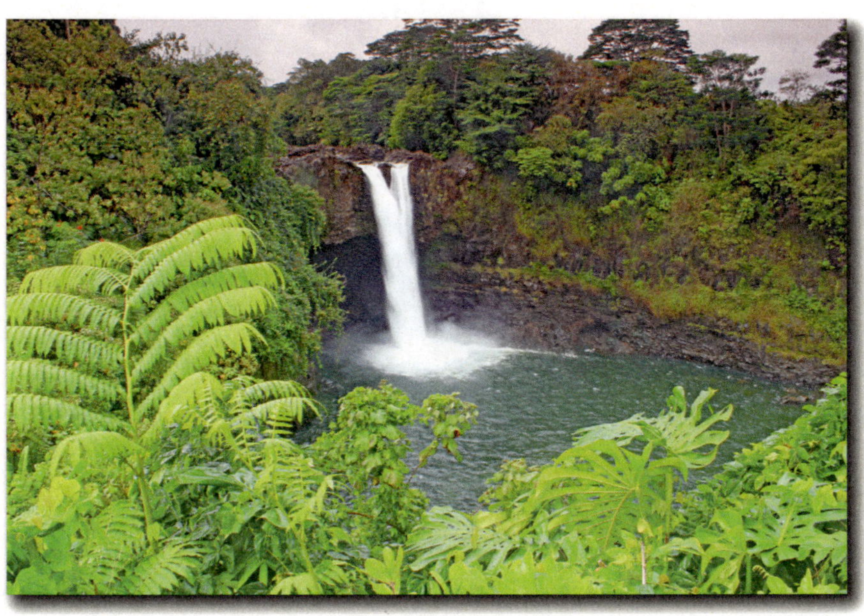

**Rainbow Falls**

# Kumukahi

Kumukahi is the eastern most point of not only the Big Island but also of all Hawaii. It is the place the sun first touches the islands each dawn.

It is also known as an area where the purest air in the world blows in after 2400 miles of open sea. And often has very rugged and wild waves for the same reason... 2400 miles of open sea. One can capture magnificent wave images here, as well as impressive coastal views mixed with excellent cloud formations and rainbows.

***The best time to be there:*** *If you are wanting sunrise colors across the sky, reflecting on the sea, then dawn is a must. Anytime of day is an excellent time for catching wave images, experiencing the refreshing trade winds, and breathing in some of the purest air on earth.*

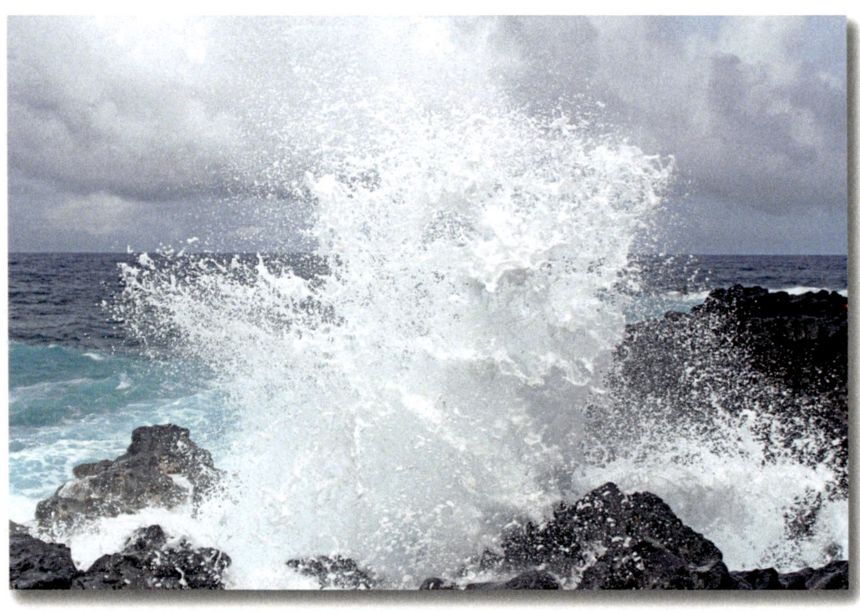

**Wave Splashing, Kumukahi**

**To get there:** Cape Kumukahi is located twenty-five miles southeast of Hilo. From Hilo, take Highway 11 south toward Kea'au. Just before Kea'au, between mm 6 & 7, turn left on Highway 130 toward Pahoa.

Drive to Pahoa (about 10 miles) and pass the first intersection that takes you into Pahoa. At the next intersection, with a traffic light, make a left turn onto Pahoa - Kapoho Road (this is also Highway 132).

Follow this road past Lava Tree State Park. Care should be taken on this road as it has a lot of curves. This is a beautiful section of road so enjoy the trees and plants. Follow Highway 132 until it comes to a stop sign. This is highway 137.

Cross the intersection onto an unmarked dirt road directly in front of you (it is still technically Highway 132) and follow it for a little more than a mile until it dead-ends near a Coast Guard light house beacon.

This road can be a bit bumpy in places (depending on when it was last graded) but can easily be navigated by any passenger car. Park near the beacon in an obvious grass/gravel parking area on the right.

From the parking area, you will head straight towards the coast. Look towards the sea for the pillar of stone atop an old lava rise. You should be able to see it clearly from the parking lot, as it stands out on the horizon due to its shape.

Aligning yourself with the ahu (pillar of stones) in the middle of the parking area - walk to the edge of the parking area towards the sea. You should see a trail heading down the embankment. Yes, there really is a trail there, which cuts across the lava to Kumukahi Point.

To the untrained eye, it can be hard to see. It actually follows the course of an old 4-wheel drive road - though common sense would dictate otherwise. Whether you find and follow the trail is not important - that you make your way to the point is.

Somewhere between the parking lot and the point – you will hit another very obvious 4-wheel drive road. Take this road to the left, and you will reach Kumukahi Point. You can *carefully* climb up next to the ahu and drink deeply of the "virgin" air and magnificent view.

If you continue past Kumukahi point and head north along the 4-wheel drive road a short ways (about a block) you will spot an "oasis" along the shoreline. This oasis like area is adorned with heliotrope trees and coconut palms, and it is a great spot for an ocean-gazing picnic, relaxing, and just enjoying. From Hilo: 25 miles Time from Hilo: approx. 30 mins.

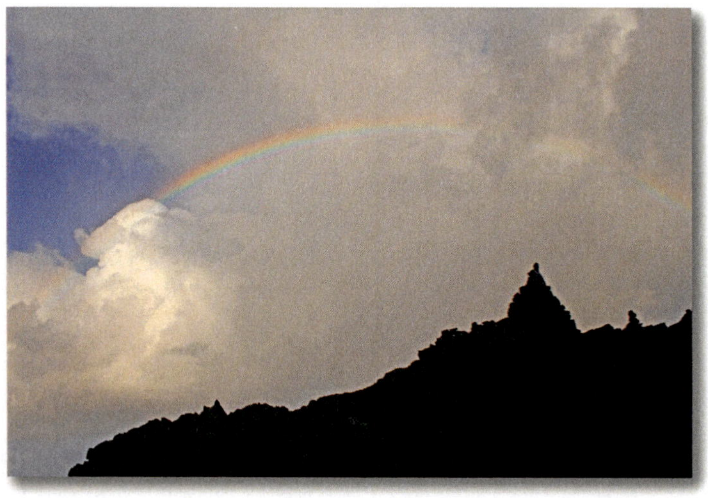

**Kumukahi Point with Rainbow**

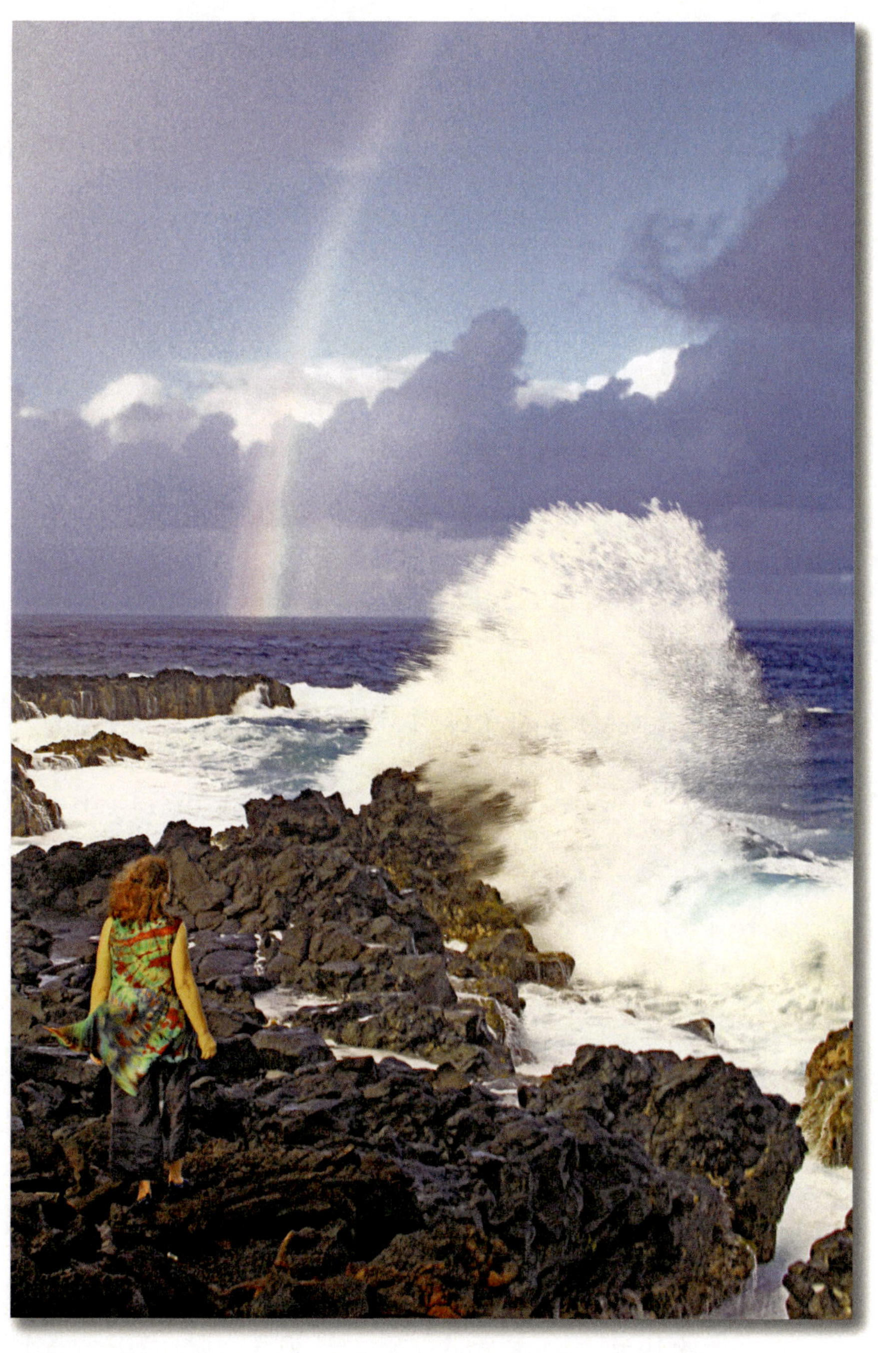

View from the Kumukahi Point area

# Puna Coast/Red Road

Along Puna Coast highway 137, locally known as the Red Road, you can access numerous incredible photo possibilities. Highway 137 follows the wild coastline.

There are places where you can see the ocean as you drive along the coast and there are also places where you can park your car, and walk in - to access the coast. There is much to explore and discover along this beautiful part of the Big Island.

***The best time to be there:*** *If you are after sunrise colors then dawn is a must. Anytime of day is an excellent time for capturing images that would include waves, scenic coastal views and rainbows.*

**To get there:** Highway 137 is about 24 miles from Hilo. From Hilo, take Highway 11 south toward Kea'au. Just before Kea'au, between mm 6 & 7, turn left on Highway 130 toward Pahoa.

Drive to Pahoa (about 10 miles) staying on highway 130 until you come to the far side of Pahoa. You will come to an intersection, with a traffic light. make a left turn onto Pahoa - Kapoho Road (this is also Highway 132).

Follow this road past Lava Tree State Park. You will find this is a beautiful section of road. Follow Highway 132 until it intersects Highway 137. The highway is unmarked but you will know you are there when you come to a stop sign. Turn left here.

Hilo: 24 miles  Time from Hilo: approx. 25 mins.

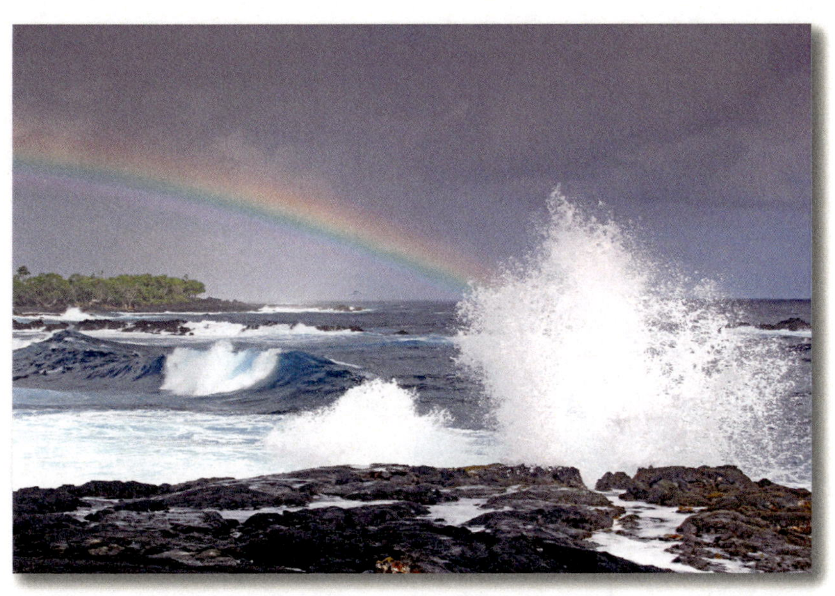

Puna Coast near Ahalanui Ponds 1

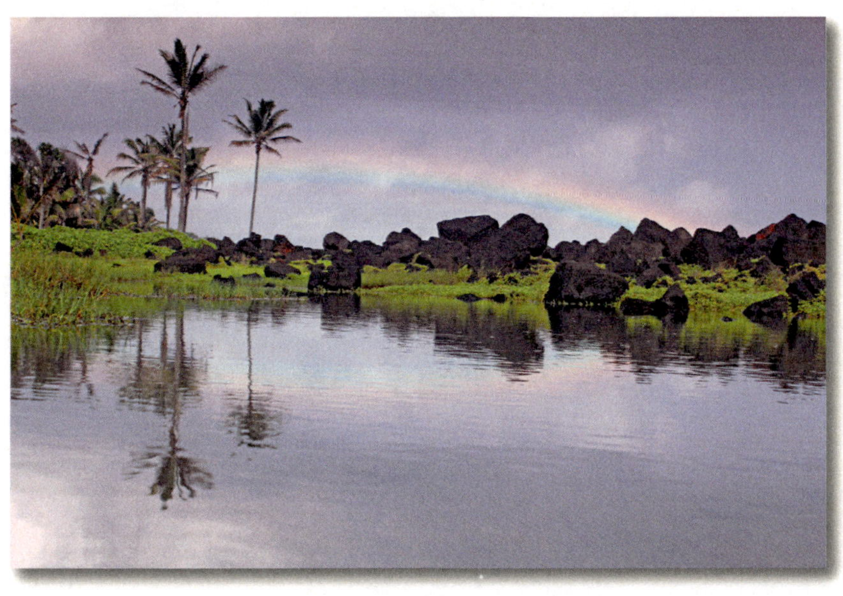

Puna Coast near Ahalanui Ponds 2

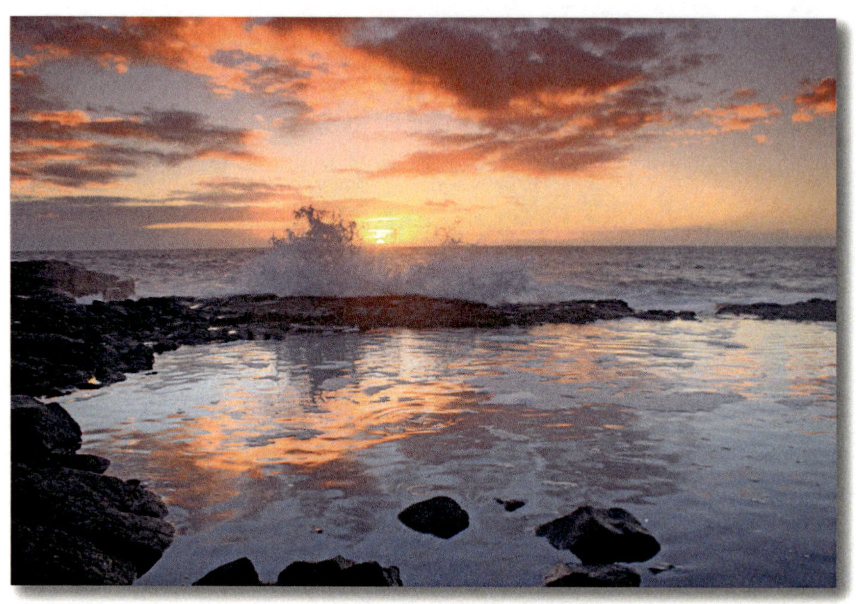

## Puna Coast near Ahalanui Warm Ponds 3

Places to explore along the Puna Coast include:

**The Ahalanui Warm Ponds area, Pohoiki Bay, in the Isaac Hale Park area, Mackenzie State Park, The coastal area in front of Seaview Estates, Kehena Black Sand Beach, The new Kalapana Black Sand Beach.**

All of the above mentioned places are in order from the starting point of highway 132 and highway 137.

They are all signed and easy to locate except for Kehena Black Sand Beach and the new Kalapana Black Sand Beach. These two are easy to find, just not signed. Kehena Black Sand Beach is located between mile marker 19 and 20. Closer to mm 19. The new Kalapana Black Sand Beach is located at the very end of Highway 137 which dead ends into a cul-de-sac. Park in the cul-de-sac area and you will see a pathway at the far edge of the cul-de-sac with yellow handrails. This path takes you to one of Hawai'i's newest black sand beaches.

If you happen to visit the new Kalapana Black Sand Beach on a Wednesday, be sure to pay a visit to Uncle Robert's farmers market. You can't miss it, it begins right there at the edge of the cul-de-sac. There is live music, wonderful food, excellent crafts, and great people. The market goes from 5 – 9 pm and a fun time is had by all.

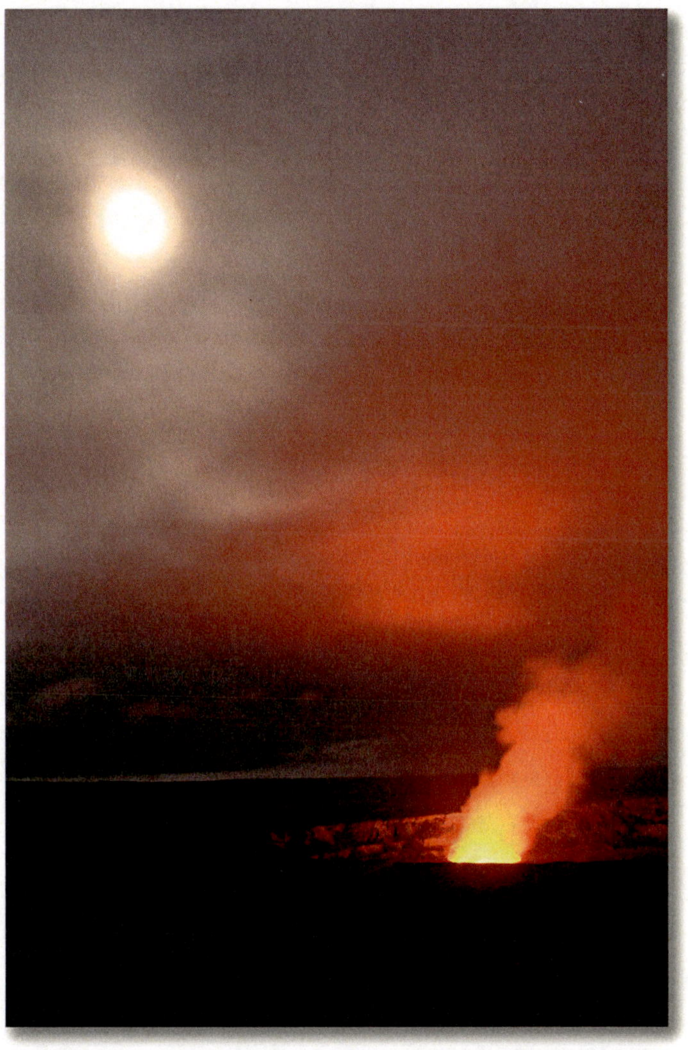

**Halema'uma'u Crater with Full Moon**

# Halema'uma'u Crater

Halema'uma'u Crater is one of the crown jewels to photograph here on the Big Island. Although consistent it is never predictable, and with the present capabilities of a digital camera you can capture stunning images.

Although amazing to experience any time of day, just by its sheer expanse and wonder, the real show begins 40 minutes before dark, regardless of the time of year.

The plume has been a nightly event at Halema'uma'u Crater since March, 2008. A series of earthquakes redistributed the underground lava to the Halema'uma'u Crater to create a lava lake at its base, thus allowing for a colorful evening plume and potential extraordinary images.

Where else do you have such easy access to a such great volcano photo op? The Jaggar Museum Overlook is the easiest and safest access to volcano viewing in the world, and awe – inspiring to behold. Get your camera ready!

***The best time to be there:*** *as mentioned above… 40 minutes before sunset and into dusk. The darker it gets the more colorful the plume will be, however, the best images usually are with a twilight sky, rather than just a black night sky. Another consideration is to shoot around the full moon, this adds yet another beautiful, if not mystical quality* *(see page 57.)*

**To get there:** Hawai'i Volcanoes National Park is 28 miles from Hilo. From Hilo, take Highway 11 south toward Kea'au. Once in Kea'au, stay on highway 11 another 21 miles. The entrance to the national park is clearly marked between mile marker 28 and 29.

From the entry gate proceed straight for 2.6 miles on Crater Rim Drive…

you will shortly pass the Visitors Center on the right, (in about a block) an excellent place for information, restrooms, free compelling films of the actual lava flows in the park, and more.

On the left - across from the Visitors Center, is Volcano House - a historic old hotel on the crater's rim. A great place for a meal, or a snack. It has an excellent gift shop, and fabulous views of the crater, while you relax and/or dine.

Continuing on from the Visitor Center/Volcano House, you will come to the Steam Vents area (definitely worth a visit.) Then drive past the Kilauea Military Camp, which will be on the right. Here you find a store, a cafeteria, and a gas station. However, you must be active or retired military personnel to use these facilities.

Continue on another 1.4 miles to the Jaggar Museum parking lot. Park here and walk over to the Jaggar Museum.

If you make it to the Jaggar Museum Overlook area between 8:30 am and 7:30 pm, you will be able to visit the Jaggar Museum and Gift shop.
**(808) 985 - 6051**

The Jaggar Museum is rich with invaluable information regarding the history, geography, and Hawaiian cultural practices in the park. This area also includes a drinking fountain and restrooms.

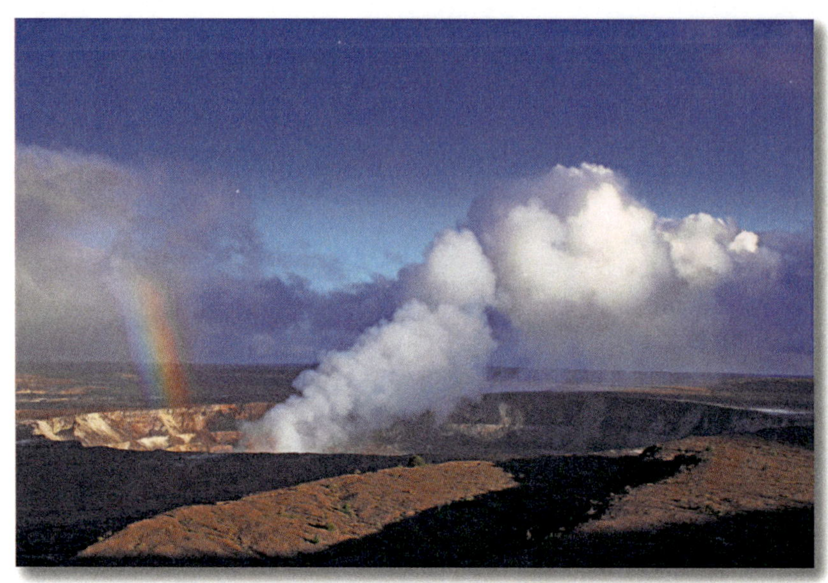

**Halema'uma'u Crater with Rainbow**
**from Jaggar Museum Overlook**

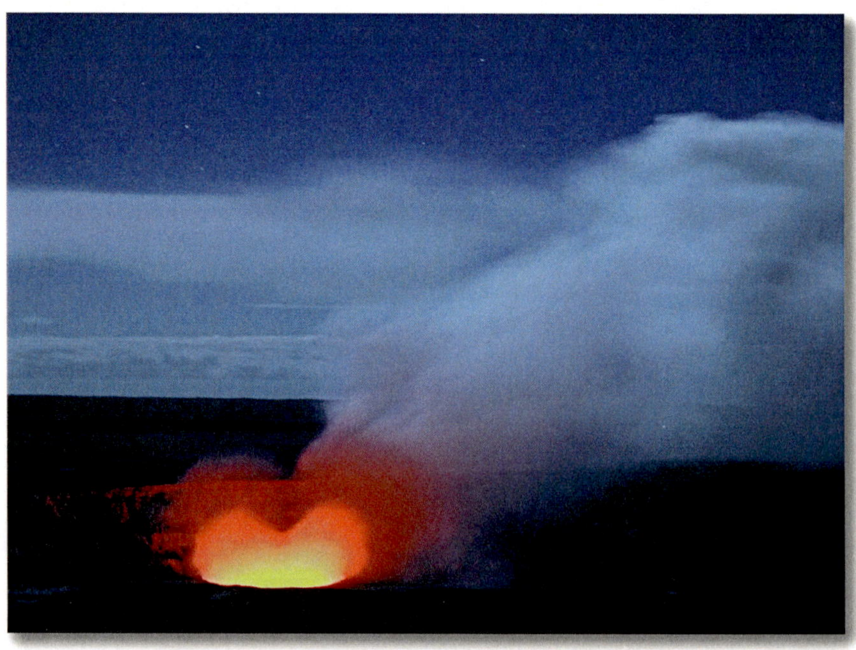

**Dusk, Halema'uma'u Crater**
**from Jaggar Museum Overlook**

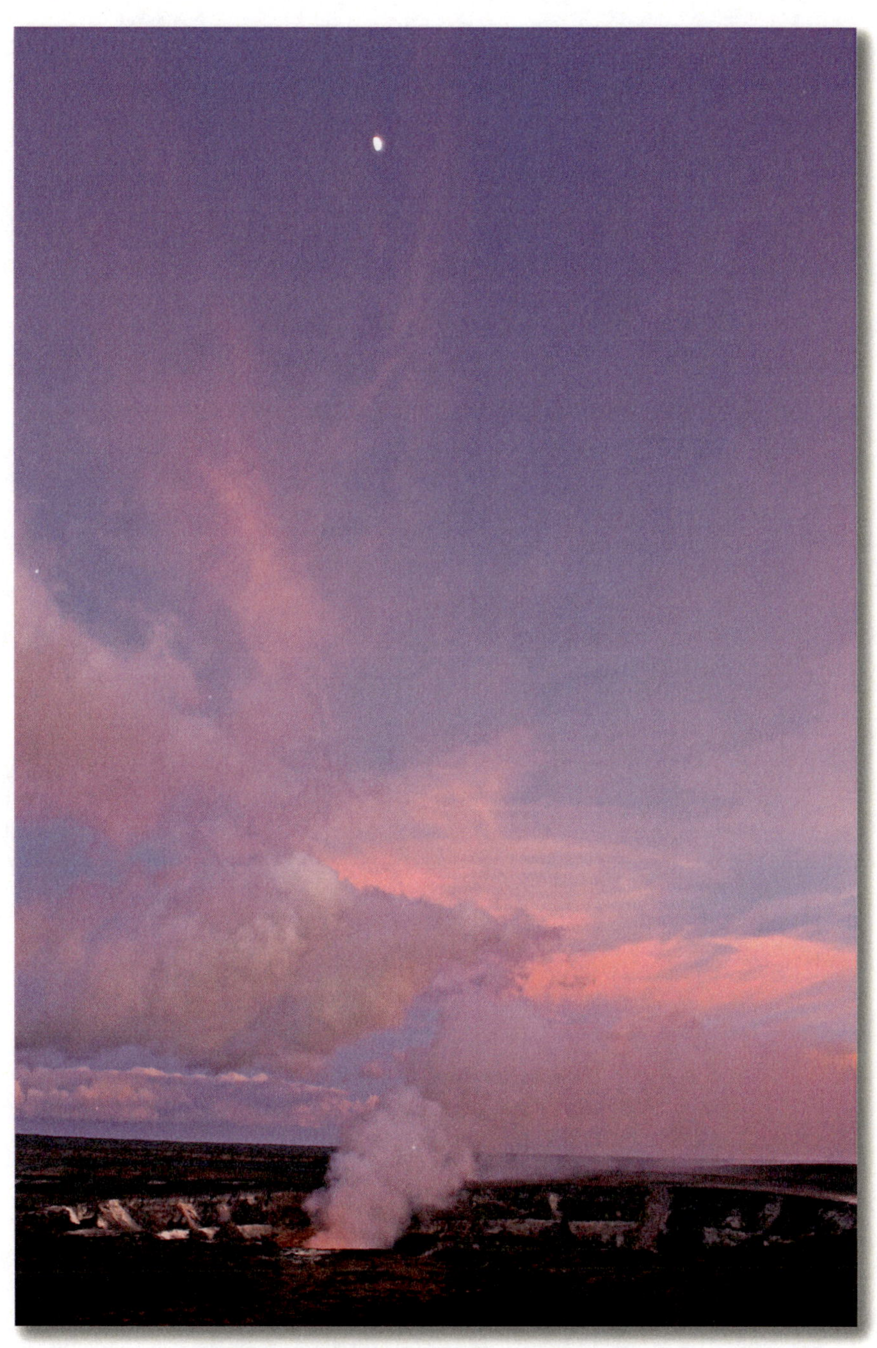

**Halema'uma'u Crater**
**from Kīlauea Overlook Area**

# Puna Coast
## at the end of Chain of Craters Road

There is so much potential to shoot a once-in-a-life-time image in Hawai'i Volcanoes National Park, that it would take another entire book to share many of the best locations towards creating outstanding images.

So, let me refer you to another book of mine: *A Photographer's Guide to Hawai'i Volcanoes National Park: Being in the Right Place, at the Right time, for the Best Image.*

If you are going to spent any amount of time photographing in Hawai'i Volcanoes National Park, this would be a ***must get*** book.

At the end of Chain of Craters Road, there are numerous exceptional photo ops. The Puna Coast *is* wild and rugged (as you may have experienced, if you spent time there already (see page 54.)

Here you will find coastal scenics, sea arches, aqua blue sea water, exploding waves, rainbows of sea spray, near by petroglyphs, petrels flying to and from their cliff nests and an occasional honu (Hawaiian green sea turtle) sticking its head out of the ocean.

***The best time to be there:*** *You can capture great sunrise images, as you can actually see the sunrise from this location, and although you can not see the actual sun set, there often excellent sunset sky colors. But if you cannot be there at these times then other photo opportunities present themselves on a regular basis* *( see page 63 and/or 65.)*

**To get there:** Enter Hawai'i Volcanoes National Park (between mm 28 & 29 on Highway 11) go to the left hand kiosk, drive fifty feet past the kiosk, and turn left on Crater Rim Drive. Continue on Crater Rim Drive until the intersection with Chain of the Craters Road (3 miles.) This will be at the second stop sign from the entry gate.

Turn left on the Chain of the Craters road, continue to the very end of the road (22.6 miles.) The Pu'u Loa Petroglyphs parking area is at mile marker 16.5

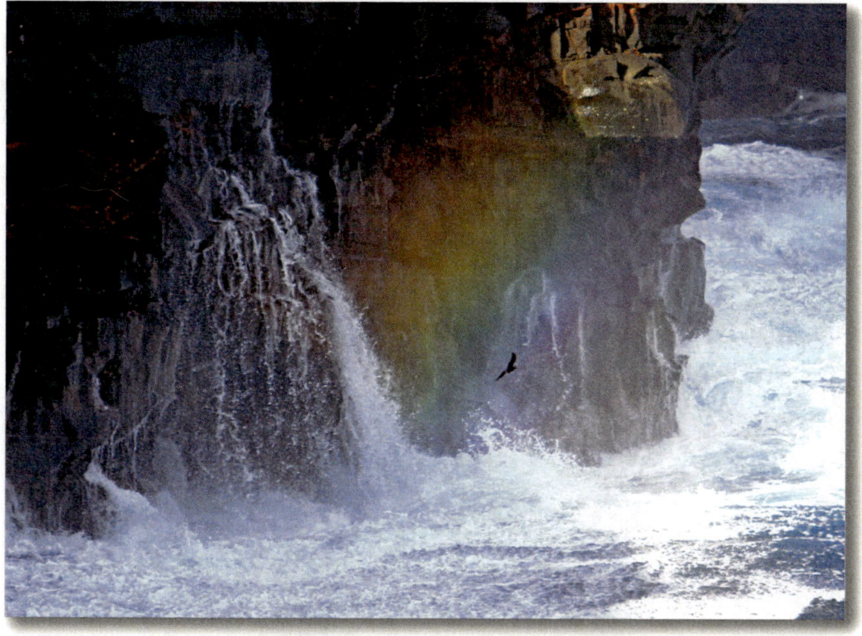

**Petrel & Sea Cliffs**

The location where the above image was captured is 22.2 miles from the entry gate… it is the last pull out area on the right before the end of Chain of Craters Road (22.6 miles.)

Where the Chain of Craters Road ends is easily accessible Hōlei Sea Arch. Park at the very end of the road, and pass the restroom area. On the right, is a trail. It is a quick short walk to the Hōlei Sea Arch Overlook.

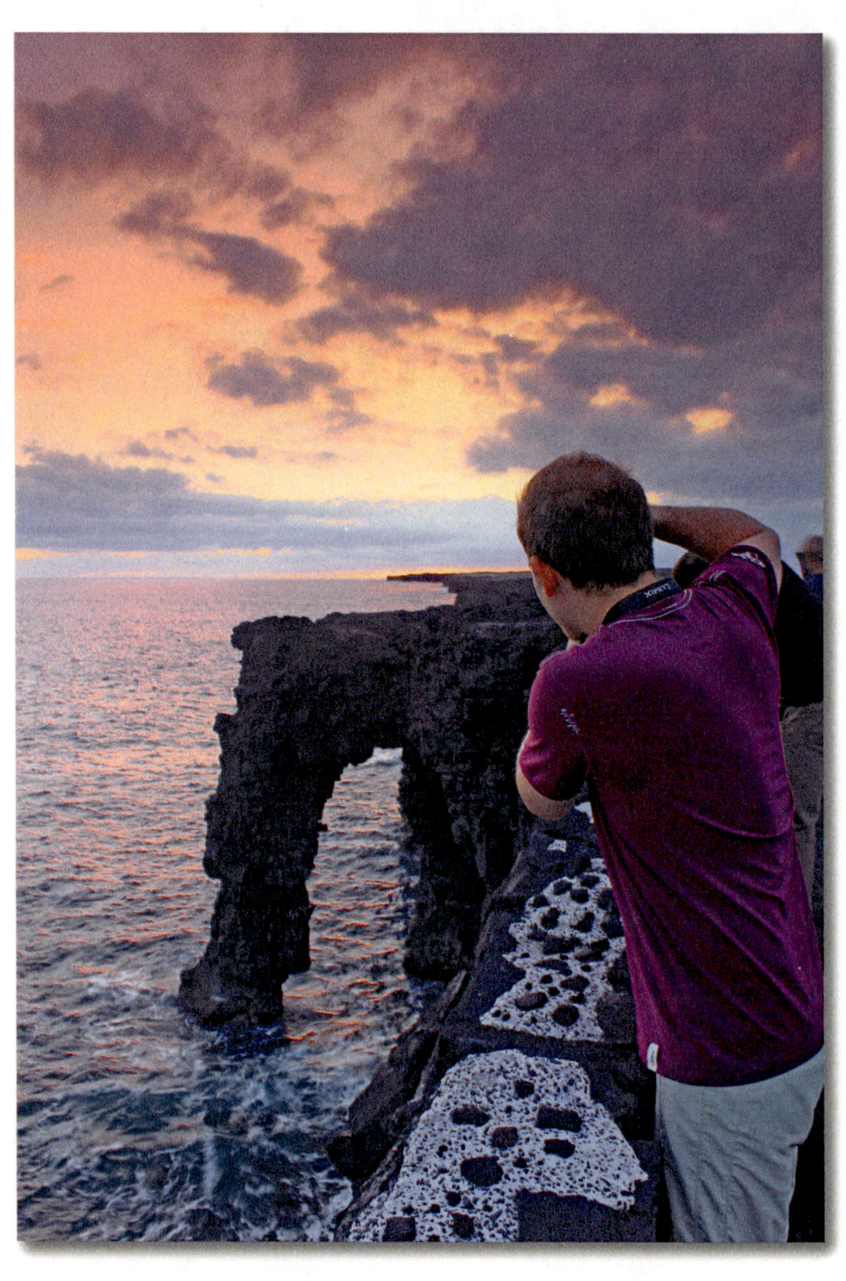

Capturing the Hōlei Sea Arch

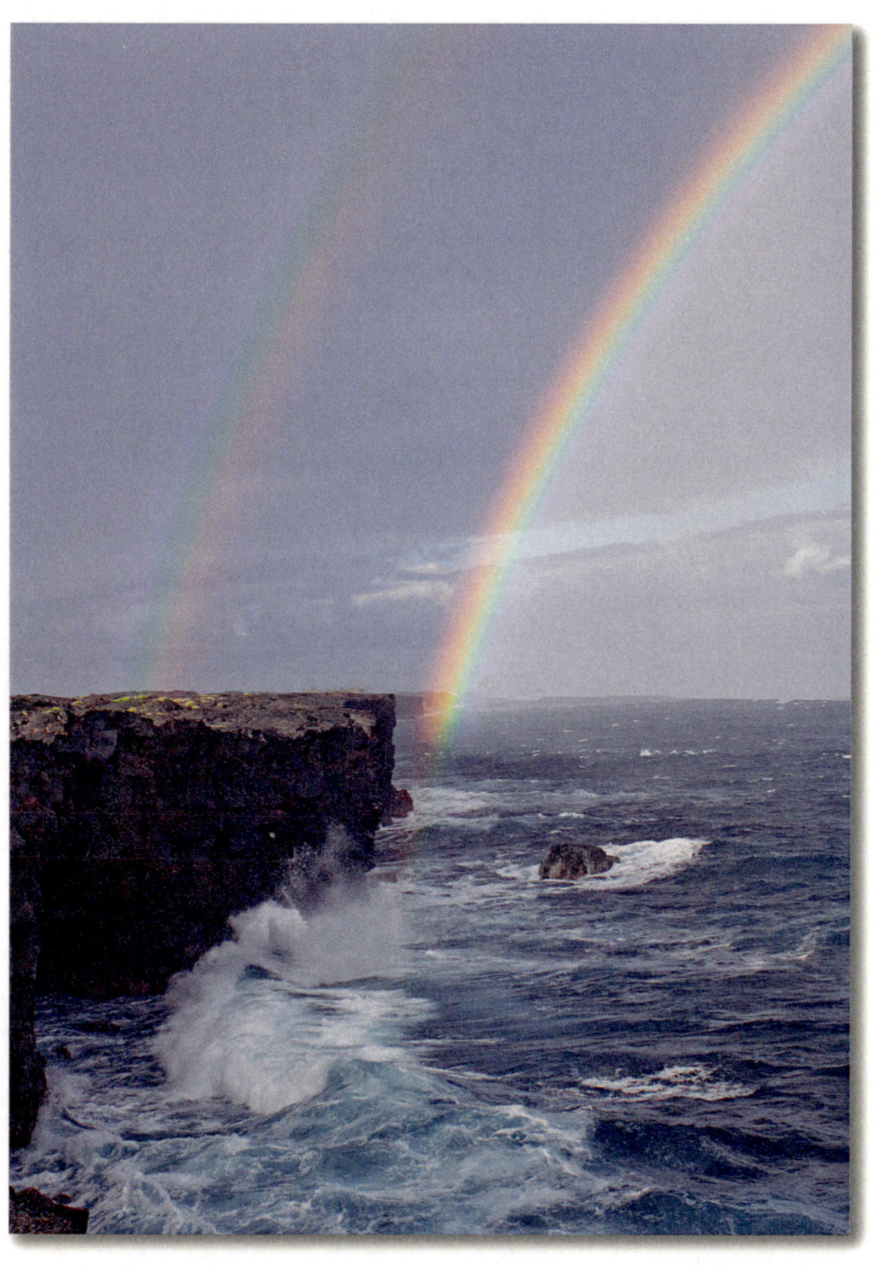

**Double Rainbow, Puna Coast**

**end of Chain of Craters Road**

# Get it While it's Hot...
# A Quick Word about Lava!

One of the biggest attractions and expectations in coming to visit Hawai'i Volcanoes National Park is the opportunity to see flowing lava.

Since 1983, lava has been coming down the pali (cliff) across the coastal flat, and into the ocean at various entry points. The lava flows have all taken place just beyond the end of Chain of Craters road.

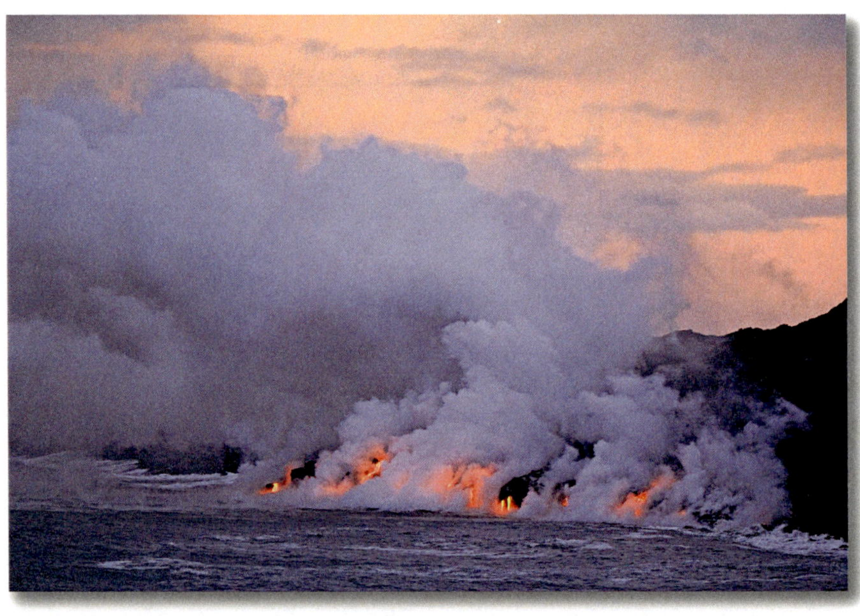

**Lava Entry into the Sea**

Though lava is presently not flowing in the park, one can never second guess Mother Nature, and another good shaking or two (earthquake) can send lava flowing directly back into the park once again.

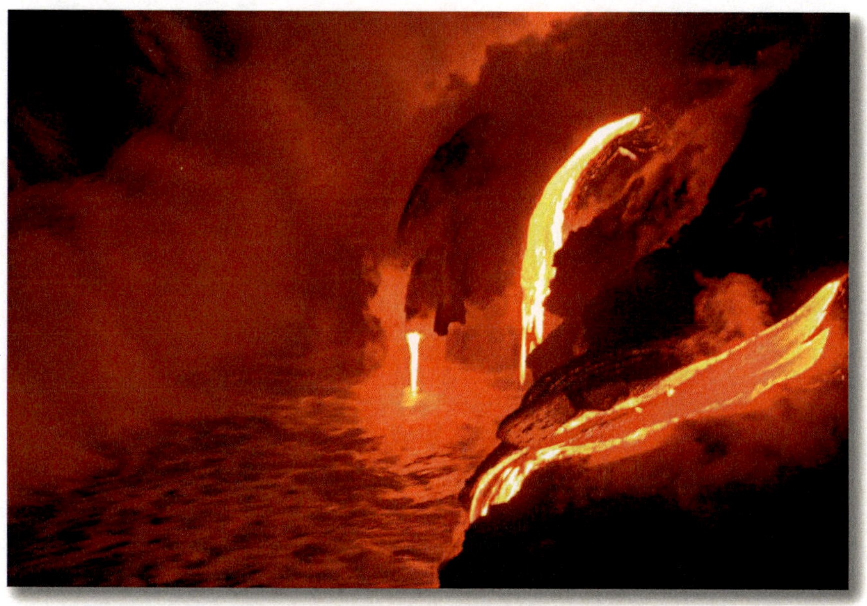

## Lava Flowing into the Sea

In which case, it would be good to know how to capture an extraordinary image of it. Like the Halema'uma'u crater glow, the best time to capture it is at dawn, or at the twilight hour.

This is because at dawn, before the sun actually rises, it is still dark enough to really capture the best color from the lava itself. And the same for dusk, as the night begins to darken around you, the lava itself will take on a new dimension, in terms of color depth.

If you shoot in the middle of the day, yes, you will still pull color, but at dawn and twilight, the color is GREATLY enhanced - giving your image that extra edge, that takes it into to the realms of the extraordinary.

As far as gear goes, a telephoto lens is best to get nice crisp images without getting too close. Lava is *HOT* after all, and you certainly don't want to be close enough to singe your eyebrows ( I've seen photographers do just that) or otherwise cause injury to yourself or your camera gear.

Because light is low at dusk and dawn, having a tripod is an excellent idea! To the photographer, there are few things worse than capturing a once-in-a-lifetime image and having it out of focus.

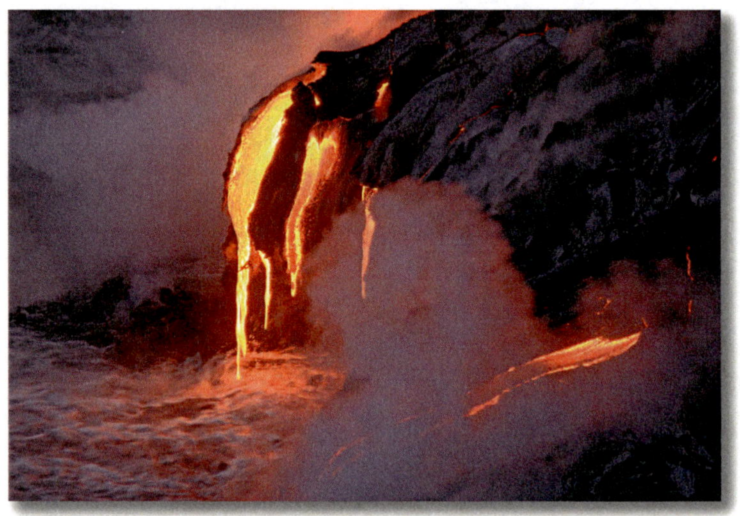

**Lava Flowing into the Sea 2**

Whether with a tripod, or hand held - be sure you are focused, and your camera is too! For wide angle images, get as close as is safe, or as mentioned, shoot with a telephoto lens to insure your safety.

First try shooting at ISO 100, this allows for the most saturated color in your image. If the lava looks slightly smeared, try 200 ISO, and if it still is not in sharp focus, then 400 ISO. As the minutes tick away at dawn, and the day becomes brighter, the lower the ISO you use, the better – to bring out the maximum color.

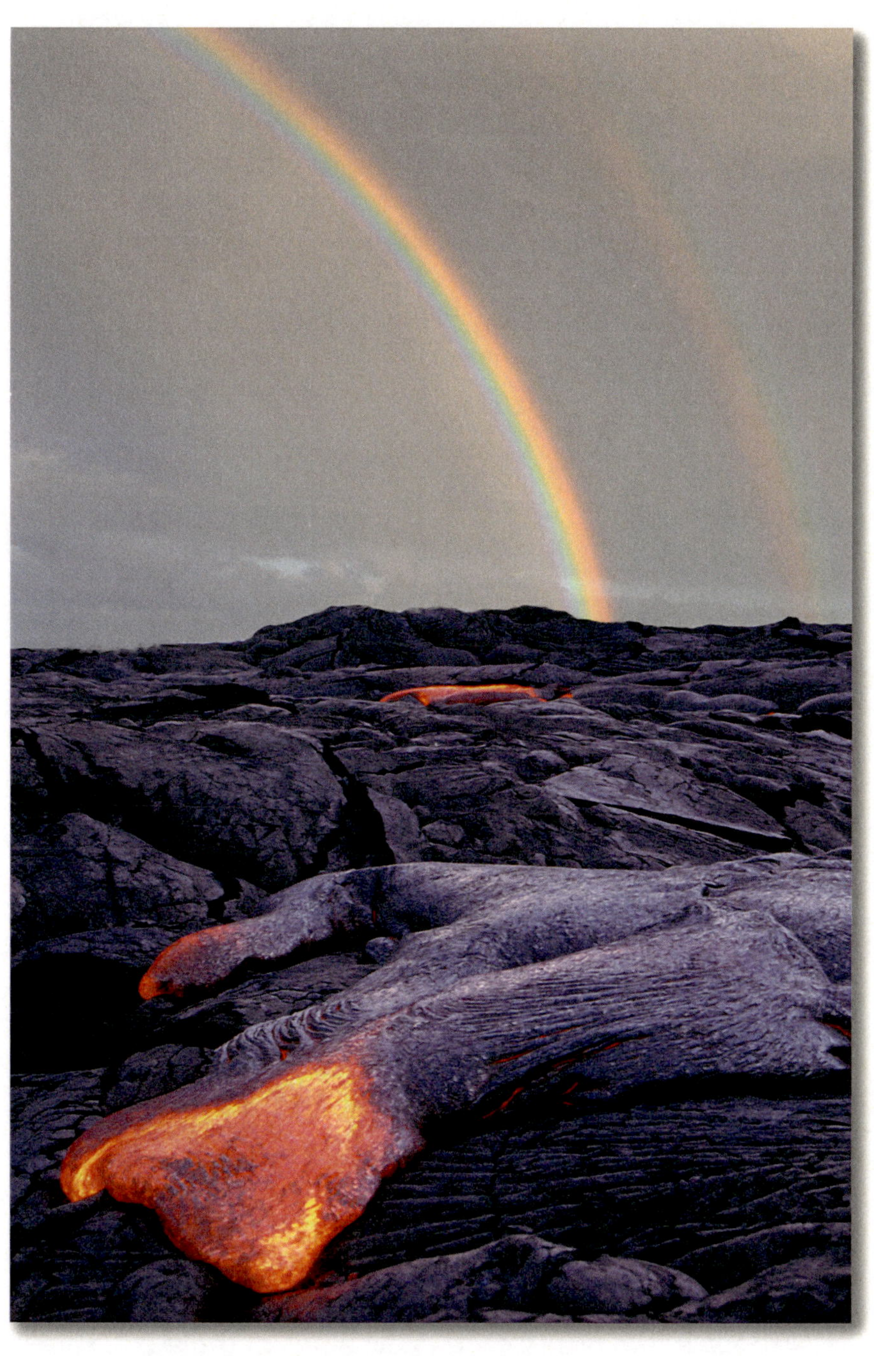

**Oozing Lava Toes**

It works the opposite at dusk, you will need to increase your ISO as the darkness envelopes you. Try also shooting around a full moon, including the moon in your image adds a touch of mystery and enchantment.

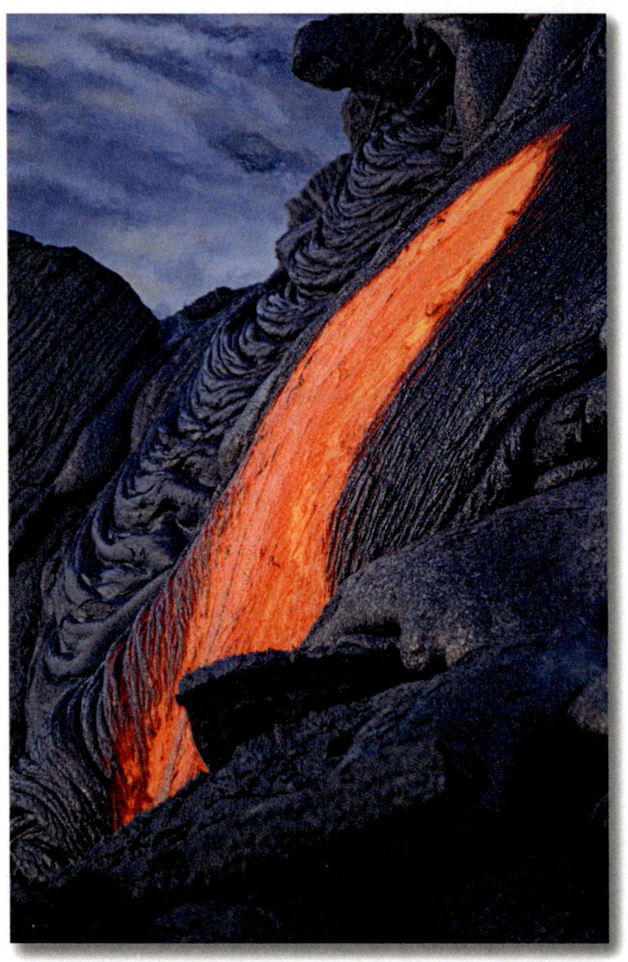

## Flowing Lava

Although it is not presently flowing in the park, it is often flowing just beyond the Eastern park boundary, **If the lava is flowing,** ***you can see it.***

**To get to the lava viewing site...** you need to go back out of the park. Turn right on highway 11 north toward Kea'au. Just after Kea'au, between mile marker 6 & 7, turn right on Highway 130 toward Pahoa.

Drive to Pahoa (about 10 miles). Continue driving past Pahoa, remaining on Highway 130 for an additional 9 miles. As the road levels off nearing the sea, there will be a left hand turn (just past mm 20) for Kalapana and Kapoho. **Do not turn left – go straight** (the road actually curves to the right.)

The road soon funnels into a one lane bumpy access road (it gets better shortly.) Stay on this road until you reach an obvious large parking area. Park here and you will be directed to the lava viewing area.

Presently lava viewing hours are from to 2 - 10 pm. But be aware that they don't let any more cars through after 8 pm. Definitely call to see what the current hours are, and whether there is actually any lava flowing or, at least visible.

Although a beautiful drive, you don't want to take an unnecessary trip, especially if your time is restricted. **The lava viewing information update number is: (808) 961-8093**

**there is also updated information available regarding the current lava status at the Jaggar Museum.**

Mostly have fun, be safe, and may you capture a magnificent image!

# Punalu'u Black Sand Beach

There is something different about the Punalu'u Black Sand Beach area located on the rugged Ka'ū coast. Within its pervading peace and remarkable beauty, you will find a unique setting that includes: Hawaiian green sea turtles, a black sand beach, gently swaying palms, incredible wave action, and a fresh water pond… complete with classic purple water lilies.

Spend some time here – hours, or a day if possible. Walk along the coast to the north and/or the south and bathe in the sense of vastness and wonder.

If you hike south on the coast for about half a mile, you will find a prominent bluff overlooking the sea, with breathtaking views of the coast looking north and a tremendous view of the mountains to the west.

***The best time to be there:*** *You can catch both sunrise colors and sunset colors here. Sunrise colors by the sun rising on the horizon, and sunset colors by the sunset light reflecting off the clouds. So just before dawn for a.m. colors and dusk for color reflecting on the both the clouds and the sea. Otherwise, you will be able to be compose and capture creative images any time of day.*

**To get there:** Punalu'u Black Sand Beach is 56 miles from Hilo. From Hilo, take Highway 11 south to Kea'au. Once in Kea'au, stay on highway 11 until you come to the 55 mile marker. Shortly after, you will see the Punalu'u Park sign on the right.

Punalu'u Black Sand Beach is 28 miles from Hawai'i Volcanoes National Park, stay on highway 11 until you come to the 55 mile marker, in both cases make the next left hand turn right after the Punalu'u Park sign.

Drive down the hill (a little over a mile) until you come to where the road levels out and you see an obvious left hand turn where a number of other cars are parked. Pull in, park and take it all in (this is an unpaved parking area.)

There is a small hut on the beach that sells water, soda, coffee, occasionally foodstuffs (don't depend on the foodstuffs) and gifts.

Just in case, be sure to have water with you, as it is often warm, and snacks are always a good idea to have with you, as there isn't much here in the way of food choices.

Available services on the northern side of the beach include water, picnic tables, restrooms, pavilions with electrical outlets, and camping by permit.

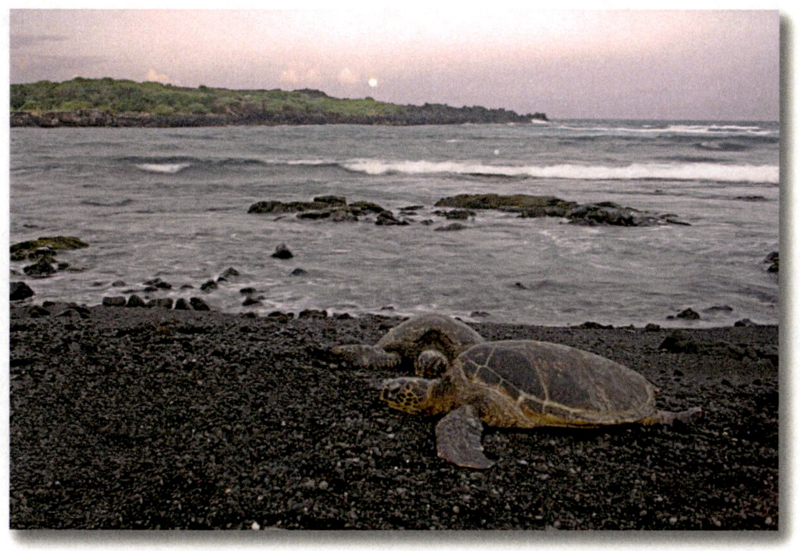

**Dusk, Punalu'u Black Sand Beach**

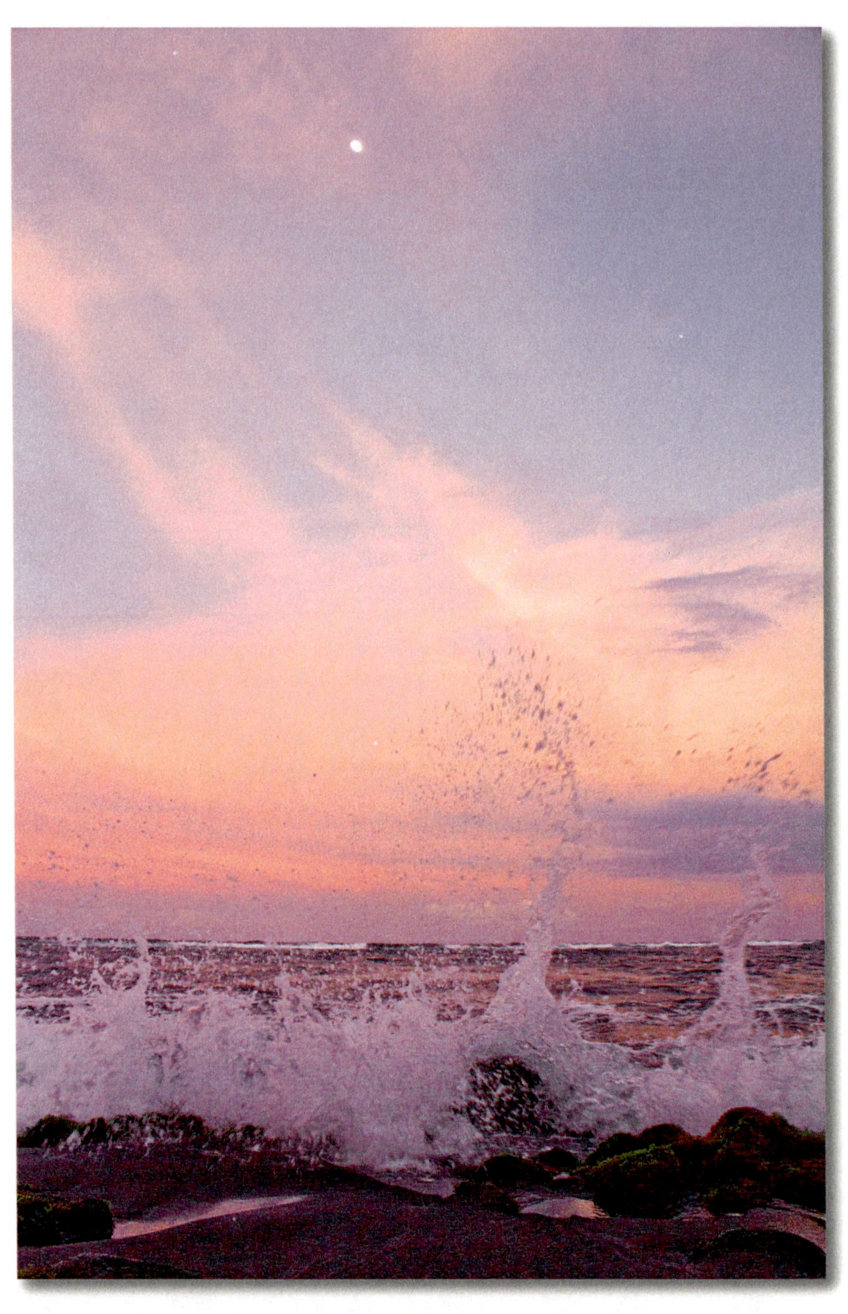

**Splashing Waves,**
**Punalu'u Black Sand Beach**

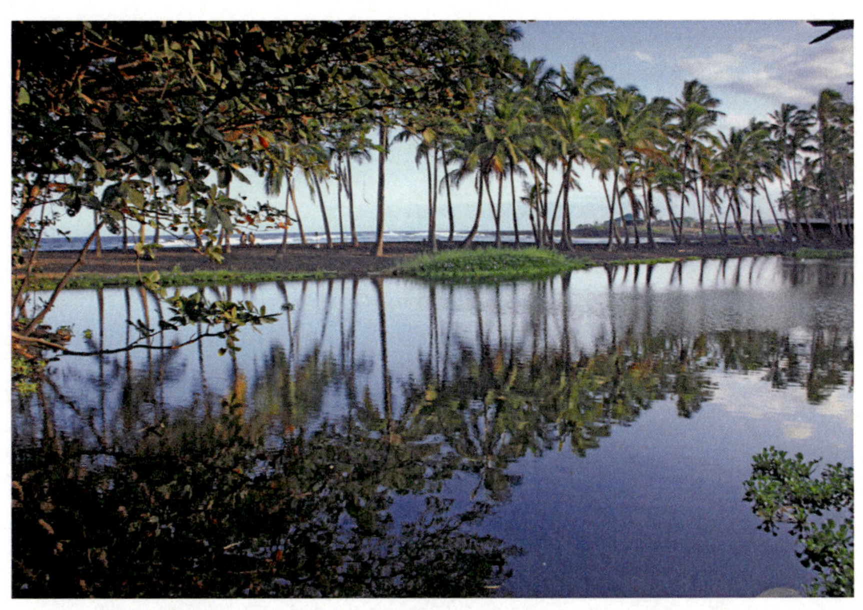

Pond, Punalu'u Black Sand Beach

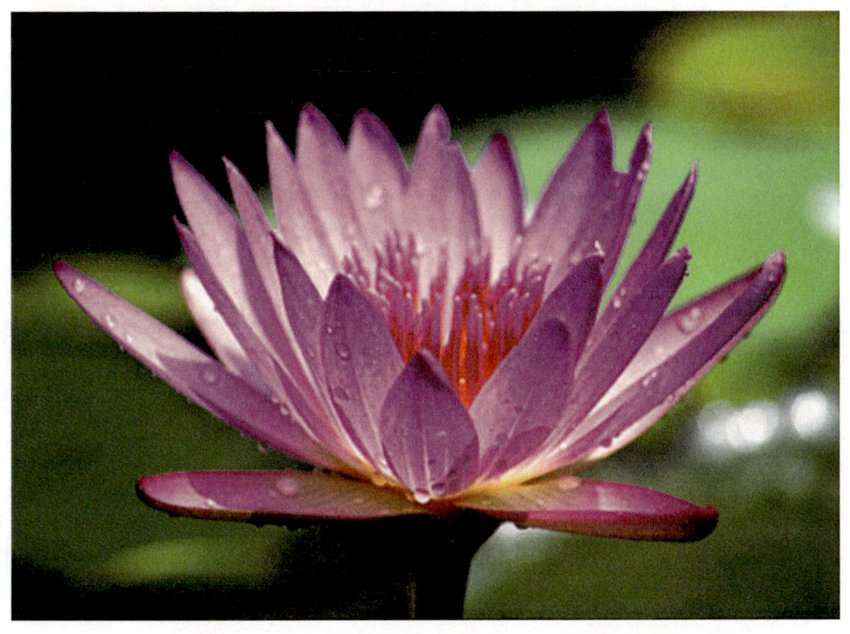

Water lily, Punalu'u Pond

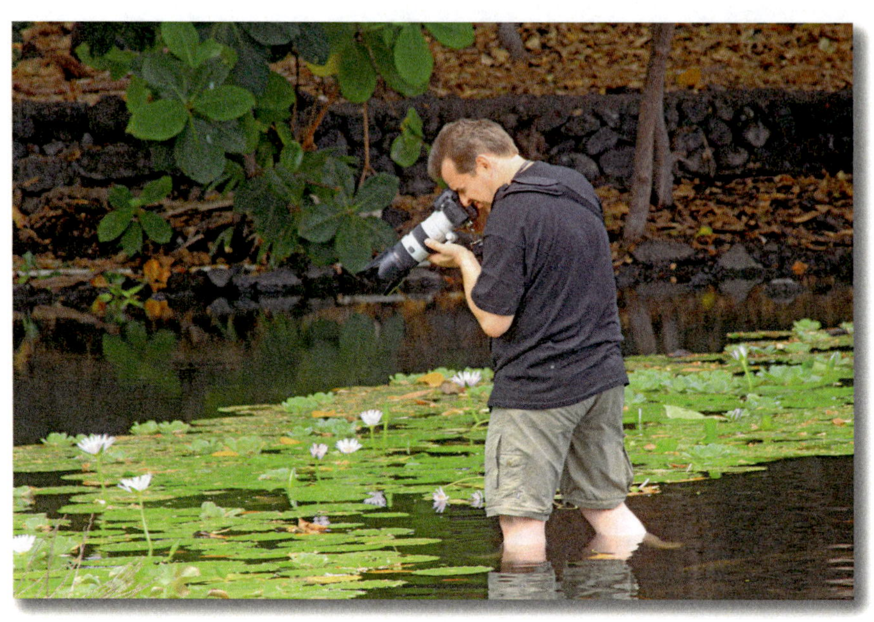

Capturing the Beauty, Punalu'u Pond

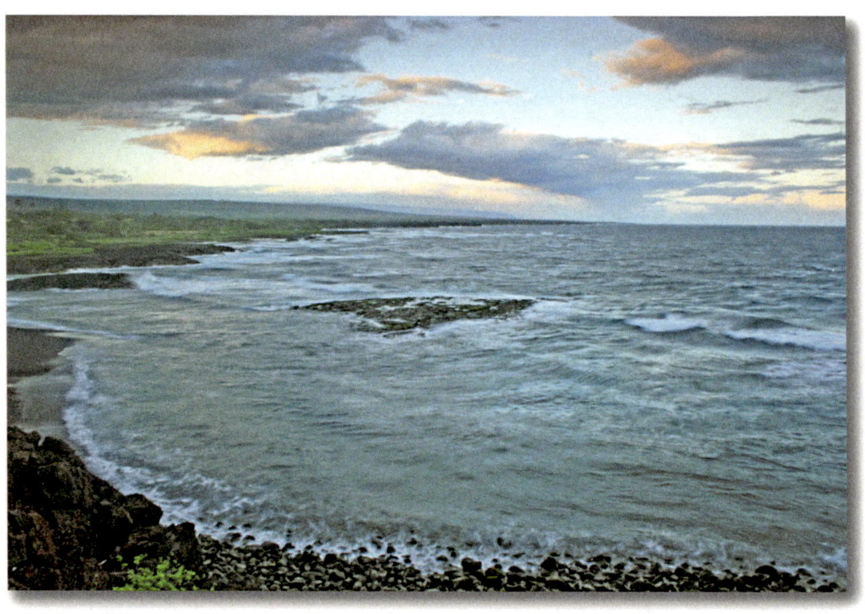

Overview from Bluff North of Punalu'u

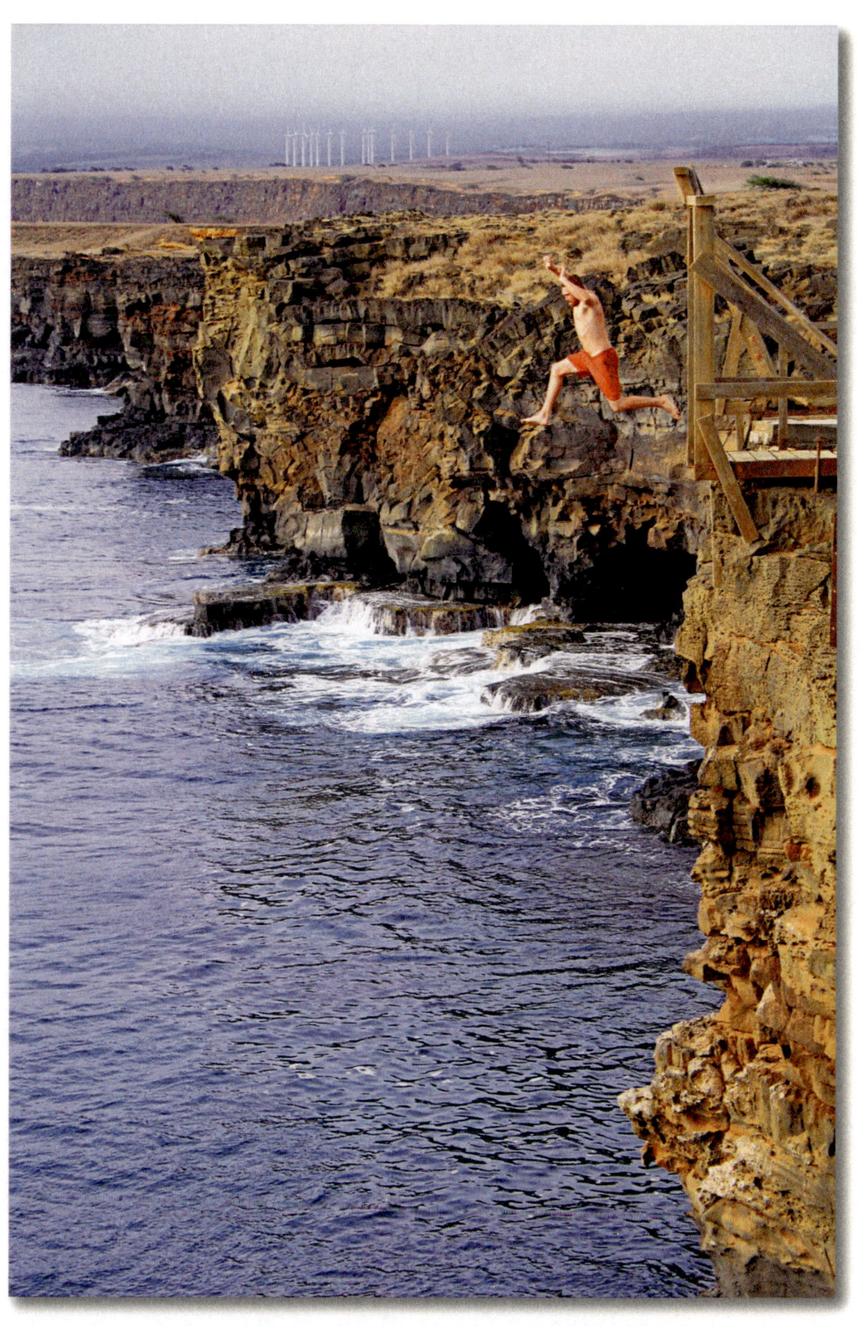

Jumping for Joy, South Point

# La Kae
## (South Point)

South Point is like no other place on the Big Island! It is often dry and warm, the hills are rolling and usually golden due to a lack of rain. The wind blows so hard at times, that trees grow sideways close to the point.

South Point is a landmass almost surrounded by the ocean that comes to a point (the southern most point in the USA.) It is at the point where photography comes most alive.

***The best time to be there:*** *You can catch both sunrise colors and sunset colors here. Both sunrise and sunset colors by the sun rising* <u>*and*</u> *setting on the horizon, So early, just before dawn for a.m. colors and dusk for sunset colors. At both times of day color reflects on the clouds and the sea. Otherwise, you will be able to find fascinating image potentials any time of day.*

**To get there:** Coming from either Kona or Hilo you will find a very well marked South Point Road sign on highway 11. From the highway it is 12 miles to the actual point.

At the road sign you are just over 50 miles and about an hour from Kona, and just over 69 miles and an hour and a half from Hilo.
If you have a four wheel drive you can drive out to Greens Sands Beach, otherwise it's a 2.25 mile hike each way. About a mile from the actual point you will come to an obvious junction with a sign saying Green Sand Beach to your left and South Point to your right. Either place you go, expect the unexpected!

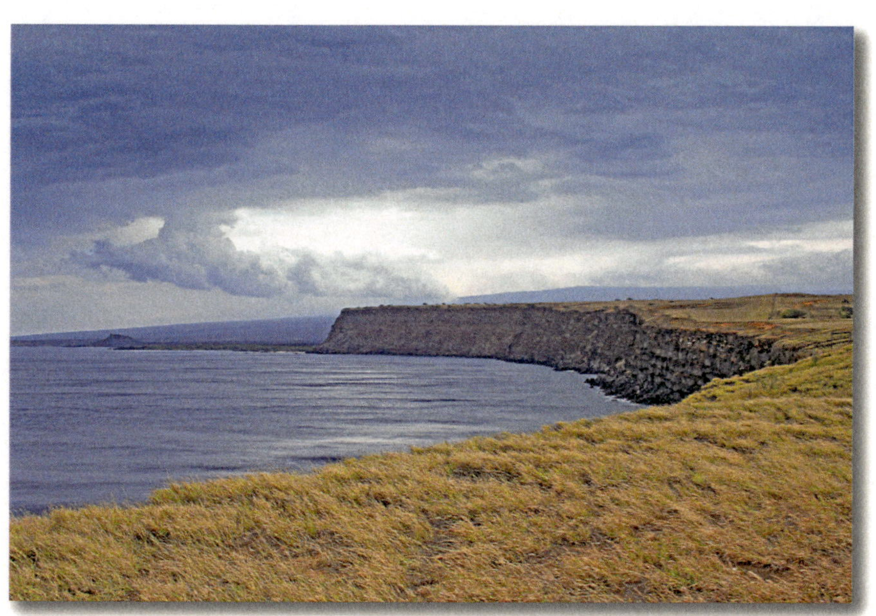

**Cool Colors, South Point**

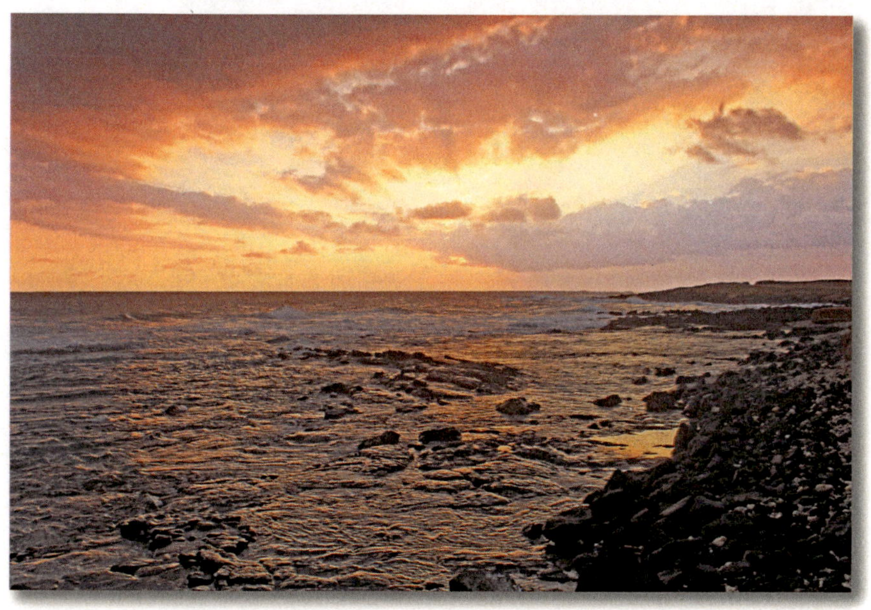

**Warm Colors, South Point**

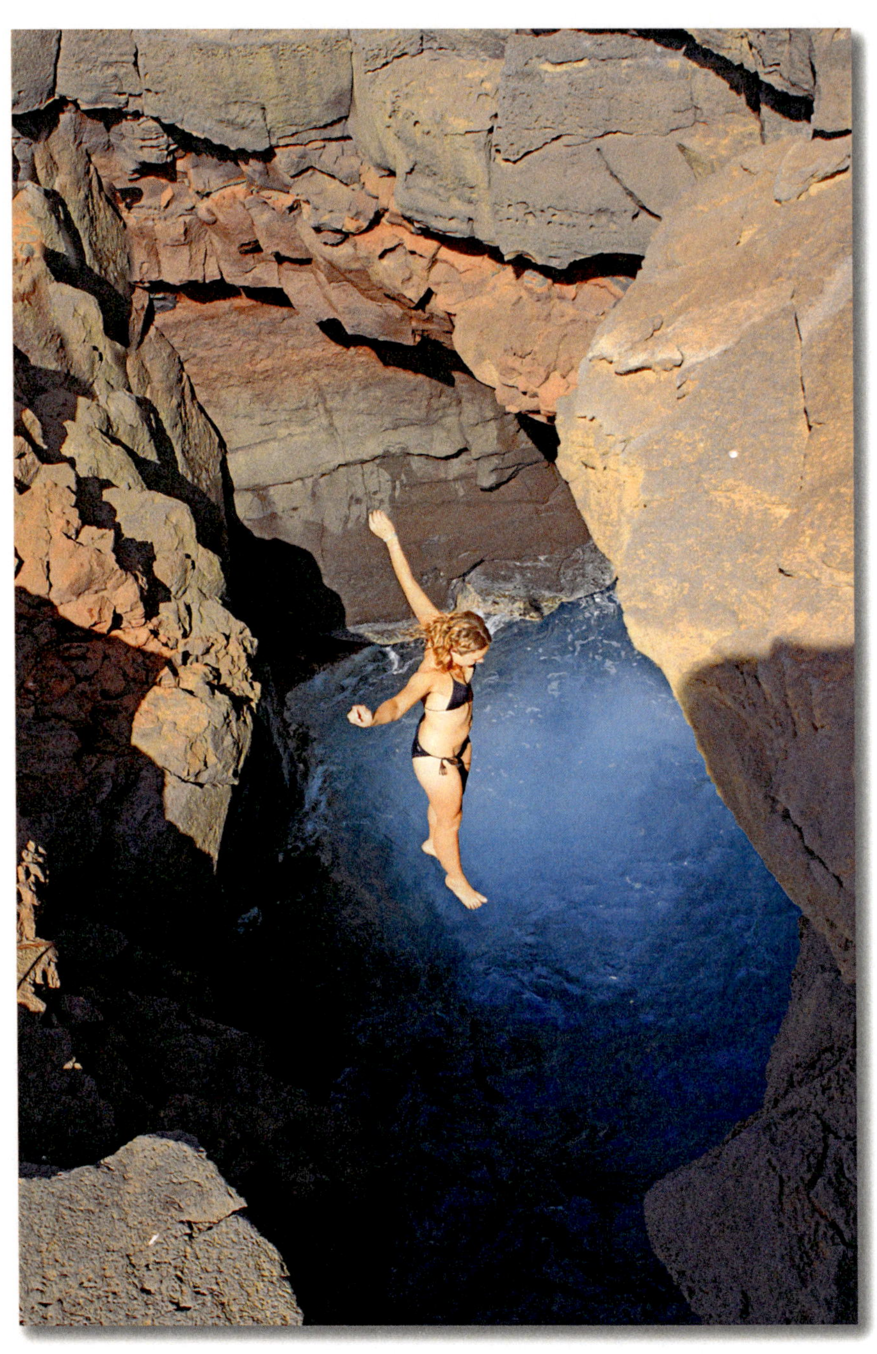

Jumping for Joy 2, South Point

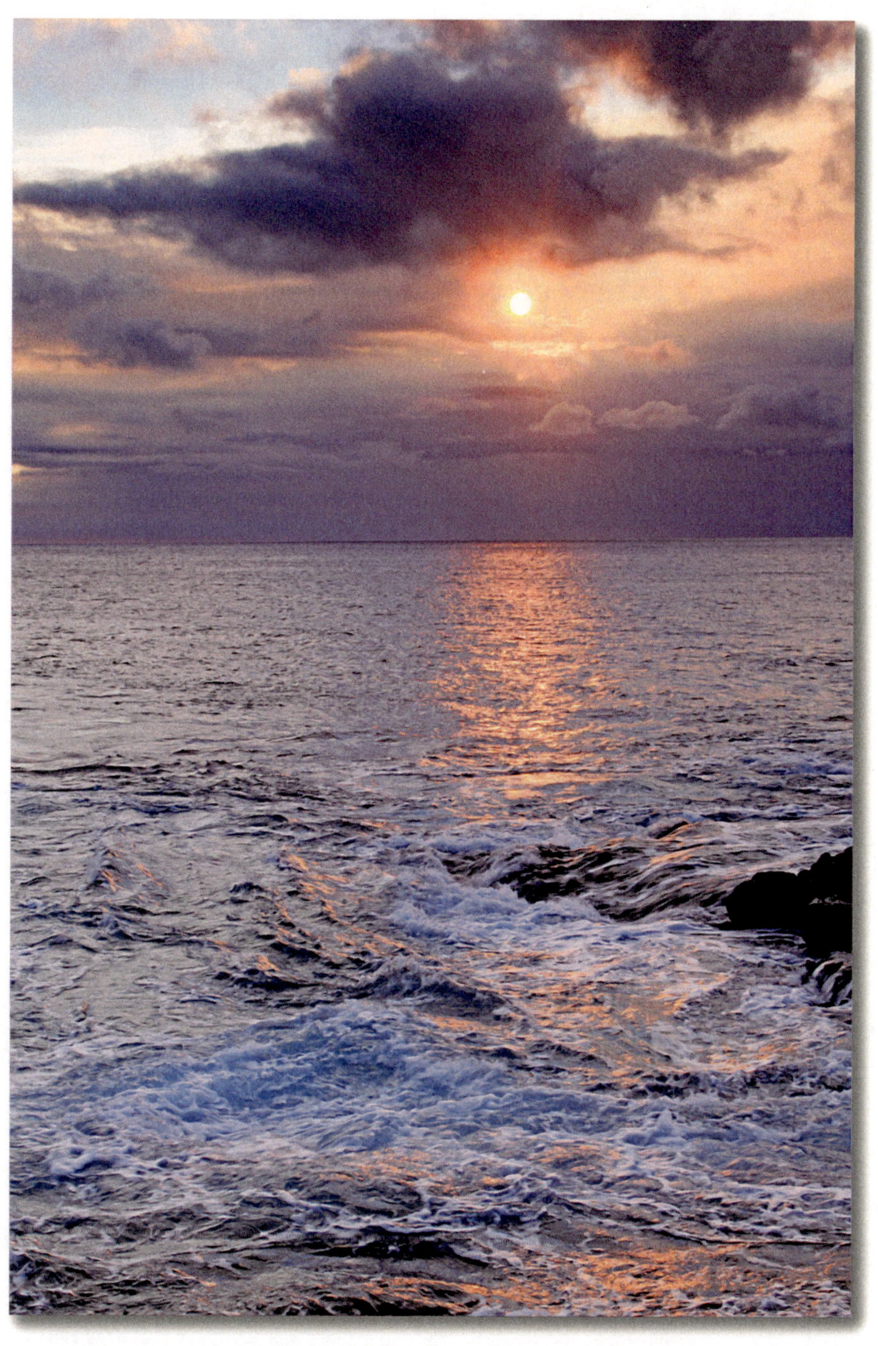

**Sunset, South Point**

## Pu'uhonua o Honaunau
## (The Place of Refuge)

Pu'uhonua o Honaunau allows you to capture classic Hawai'i images...gently swaying palms, coastal scenics and views, ki'i (wooden carved figures) Hawaiian green sea turtles, incredible waves, and outstanding sunsets.

Pu'uhonua o Honaunau once served as a significant place of refuge (be sure to pick up a brochure) an includes an old Hawaiian village known as Ki'ilae Village, royal burial grounds and heiau (places of worship, shrines.) It is a great place to capture a dynamic islandscape.

***The best time to be there:*** *You will be able to capture some amazing sunsets here, with color reflecting on the clouds and the sea, so be sure to have a tripod. Otherwise, you will be able to find captivating image potentials any time of day.*

**To get there:** Pu'uhonua O Honaunau National Historical Park is located about 22 miles south of Kailua-Kona off of Highway 11 on Highway 160. Go 4 miles down Highway 160 from Highway 11 and you will see an obvious sign for it.

Turn left at the sign and go down about a block, it is very easy to locate. There is a park entrance fee: $5.00 per vehicle, which is good for 7 days.
Park operating hours: Park opens at 7 AM. Park closes at sunset. For current park hours, please call the visitor center at (808) 328-2326 ext 1702

The Visitor Center is open 8:30 AM - 4:30 PM daily.

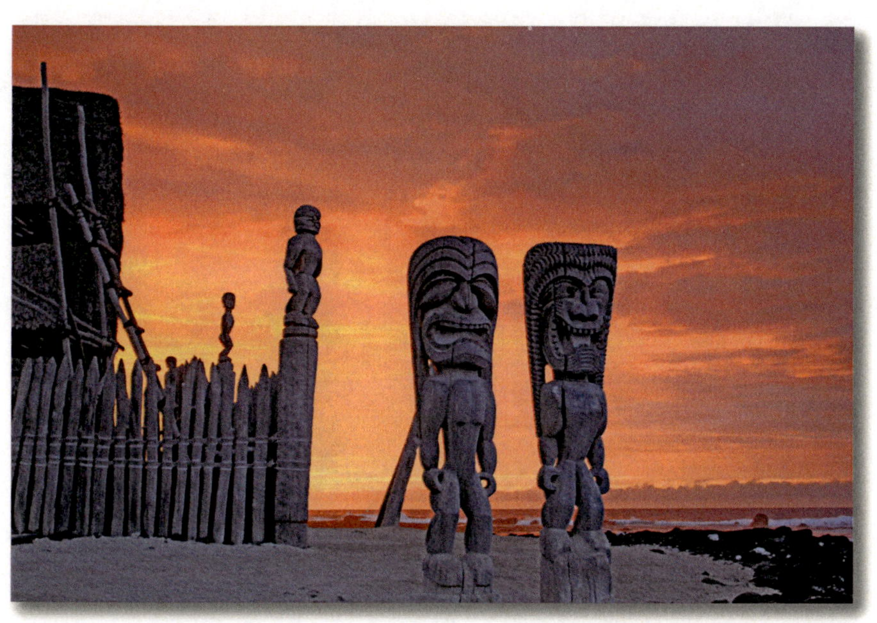

Ki'i, Pu'uhonua o Honaunau

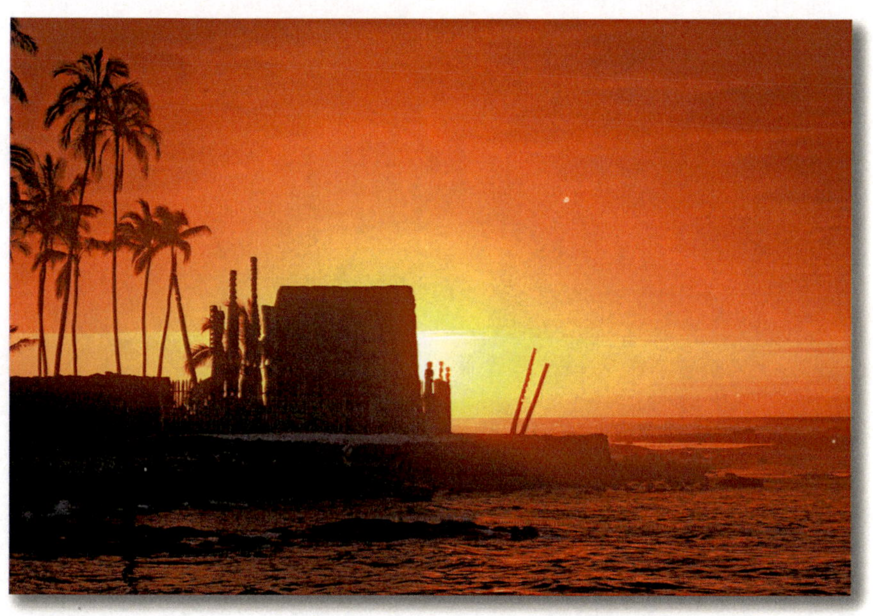

Sunset, Pu'uhonua o Honaunau

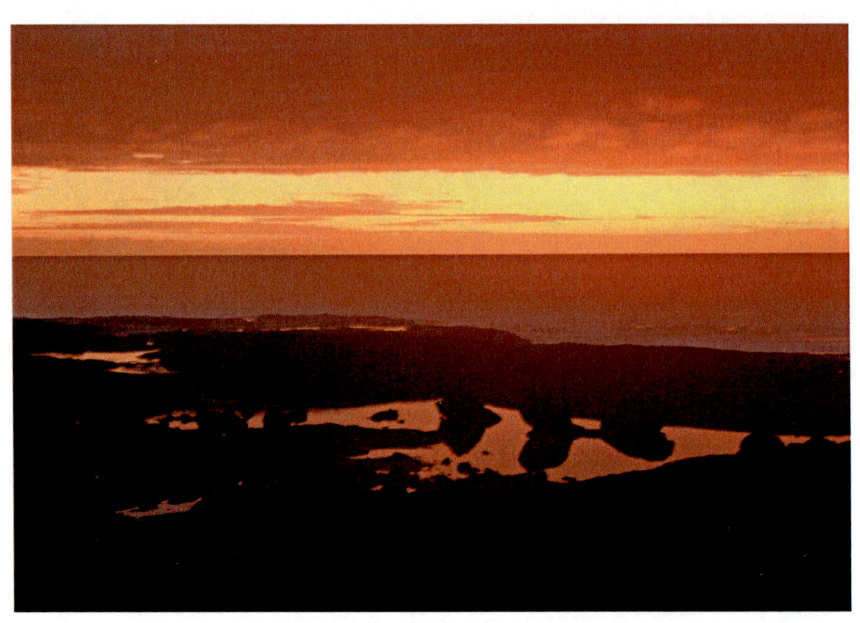

Sunset, Pu'uhonua o Honaunau

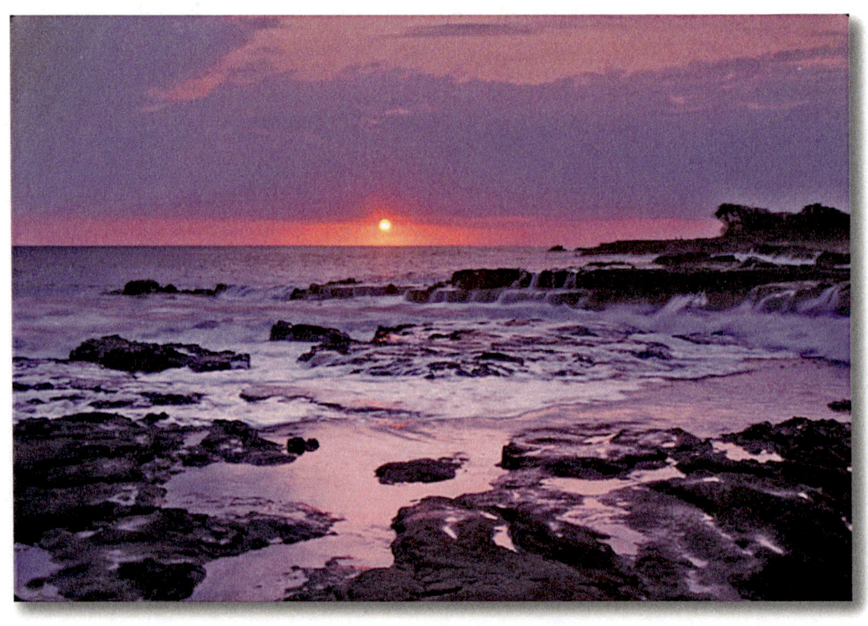

Sunset near Pu'uhonua o Honaunau

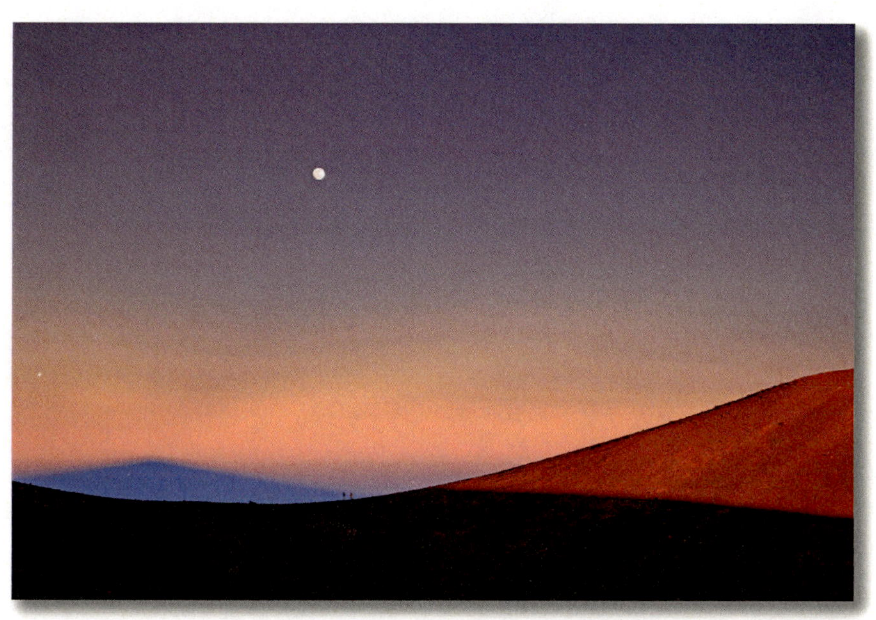

Mauna Kea with Moon

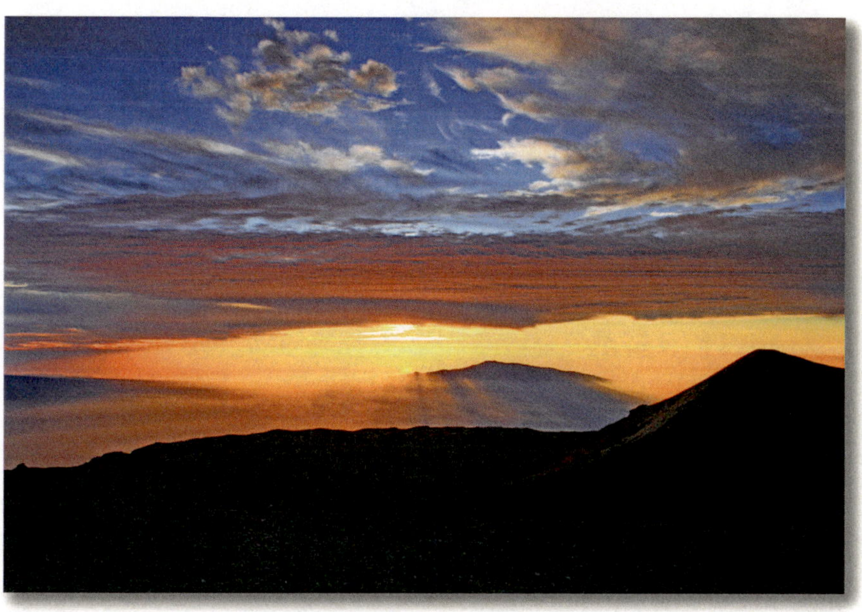

Sunset, Mauna Kea

# Mauna Kea

Mauna Kea is the highest mountain in all of Polynesia. If measured from the sea floor it is considered the highest mountain in the world.

From this elevation, unprecedented image potentials await. The mixture of constant yet unpredictable... clouds, sun, mists, colors, and lighting, combined with the Mauna Kea summit, or Mauna Loa summit in the distance, and whatever you may choose to include in the foreground of your image, can work to create that once - in - a - lifetime image.

***The best time to be there:*** *About 40 minutes before sunset is the ideal time to get there. Observe as everything begins to shift: clouds, colors, lighting, etc. Also, near full moon is a very good time to be there. Be ready and expect the best!*

**To get there: From Kona Side:**
Take upper Highway 190 (Mamalahoa Highway) to the junction of Saddle Road near mm 13. Turn on Saddle Road, Highway 200 (you can only turn one way) and drive to the 28 mm where you will make a left hand turn on to the Mauna Kea Access Road which takes you to the summit.

**From Hilo Side:** Take Kanoelehua Avenue (highway 11) to Puainako Road, which is a block past Wal-Mart and next to the KTA Supermarket. Take Puainako mauka (towards the mountains.) Continue on Puainako until it comes to a T at a stoplight in about a mile and a half.) At this point Puainako makes a slight jog. Make a right hand turn at the light and immediately get in the left lane and turn left onto the new Puainako extension, Highway 200. Follow the new Puainako extension, and within 4 or 5 miles it becomes Saddle Road. Continue on Saddle Road to the 28 mile marker where you will make a right onto the Mauna Kea access road, which takes you to the summit.

From either side of the island, you will be taking Saddle road, Highway 200, to the Mauna Kea Access road located at mm 28. The road is very well marked. From the Saddle road/Mauna Kea access road junction to the summit - it is 14 and 7/10 miles.

The Ellison Onizuka Mauna Kea Visitor Information Center is six miles From the Saddle road/Mauna Kea Access road junction at the 9,200 ft. elevation level.

The Visitor Center is open from 9 am – 10 pm every day of the year, but the restrooms are always open. The Visitor Center and the summit telescopes often offer programs for viewing the planets and stars in the evening (be sure to check out the rings of Saturn.)

Check their website for availability, www.ifa.hawaii.edu/info/vis/.

The visitor center is a great place to spend a little time to acclimate before proceeding to higher elevations. Half hour is the prescribed amount of time to acclimate.

While there you can find food stuffs, water, and a gift area, you may also choose to watch videos of the observatories in action, or go into the fenced area behind the visitor center and visit the lele (wooden altar) or observe the rare Silversword Fern.

Once you acclimate, exit the visitors center, and continue up the hill which shortly turns into a dirt road. At this point there will be a summit conditions sign. The sign also says 4-wheel, but it is only recommended and not required.

The dirt road up to the summit used to be poorly

maintained and was often bumpy and wash boarded. More recently they have been regular with the maintenance of it, and it is now a much smoother drive.

Be especially careful and alert while driving on this road, there are few guardrails and the drop-offs are extremely steep, and there are also a number of blind turns. However, the landscapes are fantastic and the views are utterly breathtaking.

After 5 miles, the dirt road will again become pavement. Continue up towards the summit until you meet a T. At the T turn right, you are almost there, just another sharp curve to the left and a steady climb in elevation and viola, you are sitting on top of the world!

Go to the highest point, and from there you will see the trail to the top of sacred Mauna Kea summit.

To get back – follow the road back down from the summit and don't forget to stop at the visitor center on the way through for star gazing and a nice cup of steaming hot chocolate – you certainly have earned it!

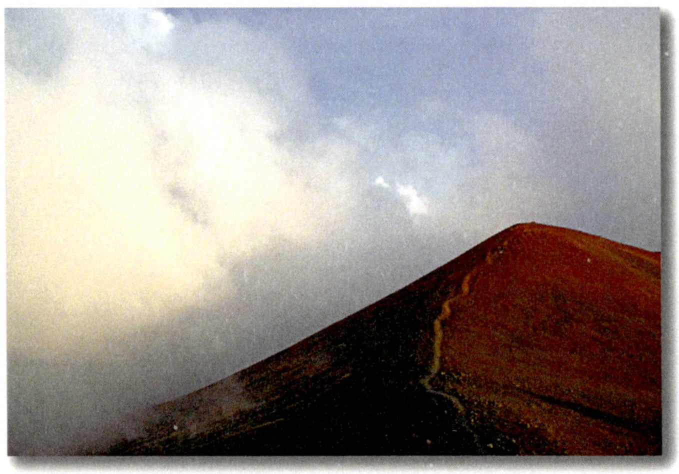

**Mauna Kea Summit**

# A Word about the Camera…
## Accessories & Necessities

As mentioned in the introduction – this is not a book about photo techniques or the art of photography.

For details on photo technique(s) and the art of photography - please refer to my other book **Light on Hawaii Capturing the Dynamic Islandscape: A Photographers Approach** - where these components are covered both in-depth and in an easy to understand presentation.

While this is a guidebook specifically designed to share with you, how to potentially be in the right place at the right time, for the best image, it would be amiss, to not mention a few camera details and insights, that may mean the difference between being able to capture an extraordinary image over a mere ordinary image.

For those who are shooting only in the point and shoot mode, then you are best served by moving on to page 91 – where you will find ***Accessories & Necessities.*** It will serve your needs more directly.

If you are familiar with your camera, beyond the point and shoot mode, then to get the best image possible you have the choice of making several adjustments in your camera. That will allow you to get more enhanced images – certainly closer to what your eye sees.

**White balance – explore the cloudy setting** - this allows the camera to pick up the colors in the landscape, closer to what the eye sees (with Nikon cameras, choose the sunny option for the same reason.)

**ISO options – switch the ISO to the lowest ISO option available – usually 100 ISO** in most cameras. With Nikons the lowest natural setting is 200 ISO. Again, this allows the camera to pick up the colors closest to what the eye naturally sees.

**Most cameras have an option for Picture Style.** It is also called Picture Control and Picture Effect in some cameras. Either way locate this option in your camera and explore shooting with the **landscape** setting. This will bring more of nature's blues and greens into your image.

**Find your metering options and choose the evaluative setting,** or in some cameras it is called the **matrix setting**. This allows for better over-all exposure.

**Quality Settings.**
To insure you have enough quality (RESOLUTION) – when you go to print your image:

locate your quality settings - and be sure to either have the quality setting on raw, or, on the largest jpg file available. Make sure that the jpg file is not in a compressed setting.

The largest setting would usual read either jpg fine or appear as jpg with a solid, not a stair-stepped shape, next to it.

Why go through all the bother of making these adjustments? Because, you most likely have noticed that there is often a gap between what the outcome of your image looks like, and what you are viewing through the viewfinder, or the LCD screen.

Until we are able to hold a camera up to our eye, click

the shutter, and have the image come out exactly how the eye sees it, we need to choose all the option adjustments available that will allow us to capture an image as close to what our eye sees, or certainly capture what our over-all vision is - as much as possible.

Again, what we choose to include in the viewfinder and what we consciously choose as our option settings, can be the difference between being able to capture an extraordinary image over a mere ordinary image.

I have found these settings to work best with the islandscapes in all of Hawaii. And have tested them repeatedly, with successful and dynamic results.

These settings are shared for your benefit, but the idea in sharing them is not to have you replicate my settings and my images, but rather to give you a foundation to create your own successful and dynamic images.

The main objective is to help and/or allow *YOU* to capture those potential once-in-a-life-time images that uplift, inspire, and convey those very special *aha* moments! And that serve as a reminder to yourself and others, that there is great beauty and wonder in the world around us.

## Accessories & Necessities

Until the distance – known as the gap - between what the human eye sees, and what a camera is capable of capturing, is eliminated - we get to explore, discover and experiment, with ***all*** the "tricks of the trade" that will allow us to bridge that gap.

Beyond the option adjustments in *"A Word about the*

*Camera,"* there are 2 accessories (really necessities) that are vitally important to capturing a successful and dynamic image.

**One of them is:
the Split Neutral Density Filter.**

This little lightweight treasure is readily available for purchase and very inexpensive, compared to most other camera gear, and yet its worth more than its weight in gold, as it is singularly - one of the most important components in allowing you to capture an extraordinary image.

***Why?*** Because it increases the dynamic light range presented in the final image - bringing the gap between what your eye sees and what the camera is capable of recording, towards a more dynamic and successful image.

Yes, **the split neutral density filter** ***IS a must,***
if you are serious about capturing successful
& dynamic outdoor images.

**The neutral density filter** is split in the middle, with half the filter being a neutral grey and the other half being clear.

The top half of the filter - the neutral grey part, holds back the light in the top part of the image and by doing so - balances the color and light in the bottom half of the image - thereby creating a more balanced over-all image in terms of light and color.

Have you ever shot an image that was beautiful on the landscape portion and yet, had a burnt out sky?

That's because your camera meter will set the exposure properties to balance the light or dark areas in your image, but generally can not cope with both the light and dark extremes, so it sets the camera exposure according to light tones or the dark tones… and the other one becomes too dark or too light.

For example, you may end up with a well exposed landscape but with an overexposed and blown out sky, or a well exposed & detailed sky with an underexposed, dark landscape.

If this has been your experience, and it holds true for most photographers at some point, then you will really appreciate the true value of the split neutral density filter.

Your skies will no longer look burnt out, and you will no longer lose your foreground to murky shadow with no detail. You will gain an image closer to what your eye perceived - with balanced light and dark tones.

The split neutral density filter comes in 1x, 2x, 3x, and 4x, light to dark increments, soft, or hard line center edges, shaped either round or square, and are made of plexiglass or glass. The most versatile split neutral density filter for Hawai'i is the 3x.

Working with the 3x filter merely means that the filter is holding back 3x more light where the darker part of the filter is placed, than the part of the filter that is clear. Thus creating a more balanced image regarding both light and color.

This split neutral density filter would be the best to start out with, as it addresses the widest range of nature photography needs, and then you can add others to your repertoire, if you have a need.

**I recommend a 3x neutral density filter, soft center edge, square, and in plexiglass.** ***Why plexiglass?*** Because its about 1/6 the cost of the glass filters, and you don't have to be worried or concerned about dropping it and breaking it nearly as easily as glass.

With that in mind, Cokin filters are a good place to start. They are relatively inexpensive (about $41.00) these days. I order through Amazon, due to the free shipping, otherwise the pricing is about the same everywhere else.

When ordering, be sure to order the P series, and not the A series. The P series has a much larger working surface area, which is great, as it allows you to cover the whole front of the lens, otherwise, you may easily see your finger in the finished image, or, you may not get the whole filter in front of the lens and this will show up abundantly clear in the image.

Either way, both of these mishaps will ruin a potential great image. And it's happened to me more than once.

And while you're at it, you can order the filter holder at the same time. It screws right onto the front of your lens (be sure to get the proper size lens adapter ring for your specific lens size.)

The exact Cokin filter recommended is the:
**Cokin P-Series Graduated ND Grey G2 Filter**
**Item model number: P121 ASIN: B0006ZSUT2**

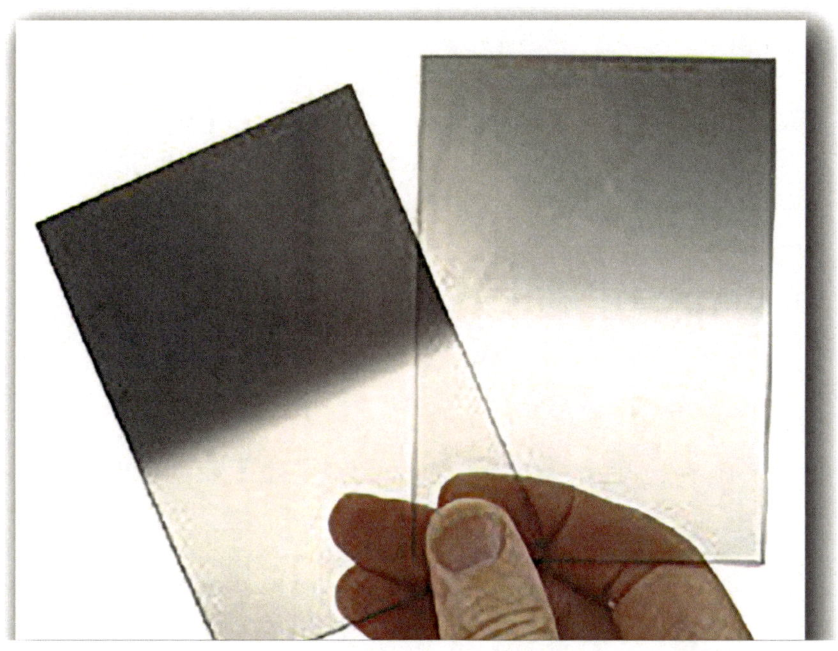

**Example of Graduated Neutral Density Grey Filter**

The beauty of the holder is that it allows you to easily slide the filter up or down in the filter holder, depending on where the split edge is needed in relationship to the horizon, ***and*** frees your hand to hold the camera more steadily.

Split neutral density filters are also available in glass and cost from $220.00 - $300.00. For more specific information – google: split neutral density filters.

Other filters that play into the desired finished outcome of the image are: the Skylight Filter, the Polarizing Filter, and the Tiffen Enhancing Filter. Again, they are used for both color and light balance.

My book **Light on Hawaii Capturing the Dynamic Islandscape: A Photographers Approach -** goes into detail about their use, and how they effect the final image outcome.

While perhaps not as essential as the neutral density filter, these other filters can certainly add a definite enhancement - that gives an extra edge to your finished image.

**And the second accessory/necessity is: the Tripod**

The tripod, once thought of as an accessory, is really a necessity for the dedicated and earnest nature photographer.

They hold and still the camera, giving you unobstructed camera control with the ability to use your hands freely to fine-tune minute adjustments of composition, to use or change filters at will, or, to change a memory card.

**And most importantly they allow you to shoot *in low light conditions without camera shake,* insuring a sharp image.**

**This last point, cannot be stressed enough, especially given the image potential of something equaling the pluming Halema'uma'u Crater, or flowing lava at dawn or dusk.**

Whichever tripod you choose, the operative words regarding a tripods value and use - are durability, steadiness, and light weight.

For the more serious photographer these additional attributes make for an excellent outdoor photography tripod - lock levers, rubber feet with spikes, the ability to adjust the legs to varying heights in uneven ground, and the ability to spread the legs out for low - to - the -

ground shooting capability.

## Some thoughts About Tripod Heads...

there are basically two types of tripod heads: the pan head and the ball head. The pan head works well for the beginning photographer. It is easy to use, handle, and control, particularly for horizontal images.

Ball heads are what most nature photographers end up using. They start out feeling a bit awkward at first - especially after being use to a tripod with a pan head.

But in the long run, they prove to be faster and more efficient in setting up your camera in fast-breaking situations that often determine if you will get the shot or not. And don't sell yourself short, if you're going to get a ball head, get one with quality.

## Tripod Quick - Release Plate

And don't forget to get a quick-release plate for your tripod head. Those wonderful little gadgets will allow you to *instantly* place and remove your camera on your tripod.

And save you the trouble of having to stand there and frustratingly screw your camera body onto your tripod every time you get ready to shoot, while the elusive dynamic image potential - slips away past your viewfinder.

With a tripod quick-release plate, its done in a snap and your chances for capturing that once-in-a-lifetime image are greatly enhanced!

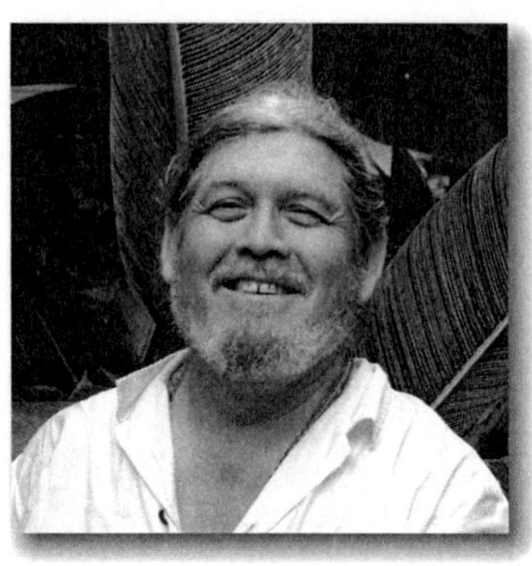

**About the Author/Photographer:**
**Robert Frutos**

Robert is one of Hawai'i's most well-known professional nature photographers & camera artists. Robert is also a professional guide, and internationally recognized author.

Robert has written several inspirational and / or educational photography books including : *Photographing Hawaii: Capturing the Beauty and Spirit of the Islands*, published by Island Heritage Publishing, *Hawaii Inspiration Afire: A Passion for the Magnificent, Light on Hawaii: Capturing the Dynamic Islandscape, A Photographers Approach,* and A *Photographer's Guide to the Big Island, Being in the Right Place, at the Right Time, for the Best Image!*

Robert, who resides in Volcano village, right outside Hawai'i Volcanoes National Park, has spent untold hours crisscrossing the Big Island - exploring tropical rainforest lushness, vast barren lava fields, viewing Halema'uma'u Crater, hiking the rugged Ka'ū wilderness. As well as, the wild and distinctive Puna coastline, and seeking out the best and most photogenic, grand and intimate photo locations.

Robert's credits include Sierra Club publications and many of the nation's top nature calendar companies. His work has appeared in national magazines including: Sierra Heritage & The Yoga Journal, and his work adorns many a book cover. Robert has served as a featured writer offering both photo techniques and inspiration - for Sierra Heritage and Light of Consciousness Magazine

Robert is the founder
of The Light of Aloha Foundation
which offers powerful techniques and dynamic tools to help you achieve your dreams, follow your inspiration, and gain an ever-increasing sense of radiant well-being.

Robert has created a unique body of work woven together from a broad spectrum of training and varied experience - a spiritual educator, counselor, professional nature photographer, internationally recognized author, kahu (minister), teacher, presenter and healing practitioner,

as well as being a successful multi-business owner that includes website design and creation, book publishing: hardcover, soft cover & ebooks, and a photo tour guide service as well as a sacred site tour guide service.

Robert possesses great depth and passion that inspire others to meet challenges, rise above limitations, and transform one's life - into the Best Life Possible.

Robert offers support, encouragement, comfort, and assistance through mentoring, educating, intuitive counseling, and spiritual coaching - allowing you a fresh perspective (the larger picture) a clear sense of direction, and greater direct inner alignment.

His accomplishments provide some insight into his passion, enthusiasm, and creativity. Robert is a gifted teacher/speaker with a unique ability to easily share and communicate "how to achieve your life goal" skills.

He brings the same passion – into sharing the Spirit of Aloha, and the beauty, wonder and magnificence of the Hawaiian Islands.

You can reach Robert at:

www.hawaiiphototours.org

www.hawaiisacredsitestours.com

www.robertfrutos.com

**email: rfphoto3@gmail.com** **Phone: 808 345 – 7179**

**Other Books by Robert Frutos**

Clarity, Inspiration, & Optimum Potential: A Concise Guide for Creating Infinite Possibility in YOUR Life!

In the Pursuit of Excellence: A Concise Guide for Creating Unlimited Possibility in YOUR Life, Business and/or Organization!

Photographing Nature in Hawaii: Capturing the Beauty & Spirit of the Islands,

Hawaii Inspiration Aflame: A Passion for the Magnificence,

With Beauty All Around Me: Inspirations to Touch the Heart, Heal and Uplift the Spirit

Walking in Beauty: Inspirational Seed Thoughts for Creating YOUR Best Life Possible

Light on Hawaii: Capturing the Dynamic Islandscape, A Photographers Approach

for more information about these books, go to:

www.hawaiisacredsitestours.com

Click on Robert's Links/Books

*Our hearts take the photograph,*

*our eyes see the light!*

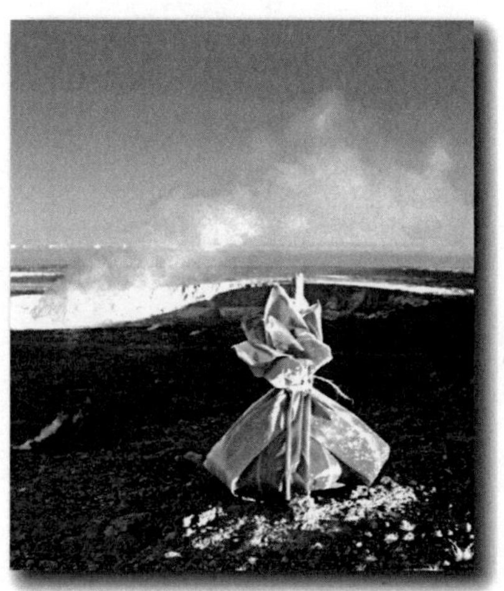

**An Offering to Pele**

Made in the USA
Middletown, DE
24 November 2015